60
SECONDS
TO
GREATNESS

60 SECONDS TO GREATNESS

Seize the Moment and Plan for Success

EDDIE L. LONG
and CECIL MURPHEY

BERKLEY PRAISE, NEW YORK

BERKLEY PRAISE
Published by The Berkley Publishing Group
A Division of Penguin Group (USA) Inc.
375 Hudson Street, New York, New York 10014, USA
Penguin Group (Canada), 90 Eglinton Avenue East, Suite 700, Toronto, Ontario M4P 2Y3, Canada
(a division of Pearson Penguin Canada Inc.)
Penguin Books Ltd., 80 Strand, London WC2R 0RL, England
Penguin Group Ireland, 25 St. Stephen's Green, Dublin 2, Ireland (a division of Penguin Books Ltd.)
Penguin Group (Australia), 250 Camberwell Road, Camberwell, Victoria 3124, Australia
(a division of Pearson Australia Group Pty. Ltd.)
Penguin Books India Pvt. Ltd., 11 Community Centre, Panchsheel Park, New Delhi—110 017, India
Penguin Group (NZ), 67 Apollo Drive, Rosedale, North Shore 0632, New Zealand
(a division of Pearson New Zealand Ltd.)
Penguin Books (South Africa) (Pty.) Ltd., 24 Sturdee Avenue, Rosebank, Johannesburg 2196,
South Africa

Penguin Books Ltd., Registered Offices: 80 Strand, London WC2R 0RL, England

This book is an original publication of The Berkley Publishing Group.

Unless otherwise noted, all Scripture references are taken from the New King James Version (NKJV) of the Bible. Copyright © 1982 by Thomas Nelson, Inc., Publishers. Others are: KJV—taken from the King James Version of the Bible. Copyright © 1979, 1980, 1982 by Thomas Nelson, Inc., Publishers. NIV—taken from the Holy Bible, New International Version. Copyright © 1973, 1978, 1984 International Bible Society. Used by permission of Zondervan Bible Publishers. NLT—taken from the Holy Bible, New Living Translation, copyright © 1996, 2004. Used by permission of Tyndale House Publishers, Inc., Wheaton, Illinois 60189. All rights reserved. *The Message* copyright © 1993, 1994, 1995, 1996, 2000, 2001, 2002. Used by permission of NavPress Publishing Group.

The publisher does not have any control over and does not assume any responsibility for author or third-party websites or their content.

FIRST EDITION: January 2010

Library of Congress Cataloging-in-Publication Data

Long, Eddie.
    60 seconds to greatness : seize the moment and plan for success / Eddie L. Long and Cecil Murphey. — 1st ed.
        p.   cm.
    ISBN 978-0-425-22161-7
    1. Success—Religious aspects—Christianity.   I. Murphey, Cecil B.   II. Title.   III. Title: Sixty seconds to greatness.
BV4598.3.L66 2010
    248.4—dc22
    2009029960

PRINTED IN THE UNITED STATES OF AMERICA

10   9   8   7   6   5   4   3   2

I have only just a minute, only 60 seconds in it,
Forced upon me, can't refuse it.
Didn't seek it, didn't choose it,
But it's up to me to use it.
I must suffer if I lose it,
Give account if I abuse it.
Just a tiny little minute,
But eternity is in it.
What are you going to do with your minute?

—Attributed to Dr. Benjamin Mays (1894–1984)

CONTENTS

1

The Value of

60 SECONDS

Think about the value of 60 seconds—that's exactly one minute of your time. You can waste your life as you watch those seconds tick away so easily. Or you can realize that they are valuable and during those seconds your life can change.

You no longer have to live a defeated life, wondering where you're going and what lies ahead. You can make a decision during the next 60 seconds that not only will change your life, but that decision can lead you to greatness.

Greatness? Yes, that's exactly the word I used.

Greatness may not be fame or immense wealth. It may not mean having the world know who you are, but there are other kinds of greatness. For example, you can change your children and your children's children and the generations that follow them. And it can all be traced back to you and the choice that you made.

Greatness starts with a choice. A decision.

You can decide to be great.

It starts when you realize the value of each 60 seconds in your life.

Here's something for you to think about: Actress Halle Berry makes $30 a minute because of who she is. Tiger Woods makes $175 a minute because of what he does. Steven Spielberg earns $675 a minute because of what he gets others to do. Bill Gates is worth more than $6,500 a minute because of what he gets the world to do.

Those are extreme examples, and they're all about money. But you can use your seconds to turn your life into great value. Just think: *You can change your life in 60 seconds.* You can start a journey to become someone you've never been before. You can move from defeated, poverty-level living to victorious, prosperity-rich living. Only you can make that choice.

Each of us operates with seconds that add up to minutes to hours to days to months and to years. Most of us pay little attention to the seconds that tick away in our lives. Only when we become aware of how much time has passed do we awaken, shake our heads, and wonder how so much time has gone by with so little accomplished.

Those seconds are important.

It's not the monetary value of time that's most important. It's the inner value, the deeper values that make your life more meaningful. Jesus Christ gave what we call the Great Commission to make disciples of all nations. That commission empowers us and teaches us to become everything God wants us to become.

And it can begin during the next 60 seconds. It can begin for anyone. It can begin for you. Right now.

I can teach you to follow the principles that will change your life and, in the process, empower you. The more people I empower, the more valuable each of my minutes becomes. Their minutes are tied up in my minutes. By that I mean I can teach other people and guide them (and so can you) and they become more valuable to themselves and to society. As others become more valuable to the world, that adds value to my minutes.

Here's an example. A good friend, Dr. Samuel Chand, wanted to become involved in building leadership. Sam didn't know if he could succeed. He looked at himself (which is always a good place to start) and at his abilities and liabilities. He had come from India at age eighteen, gone to college, earned a few degrees, and eventually he became the president of Beulah Heights University. People know him as a powerful innovator and developer of leaders.

Most of them don't know that he started where most of you begin. He wanted to teach leadership tactics and principles but he wasn't sure he could do it. Sam didn't sit around and wonder, but he made a decision to try. He was willing to fail if he had to, but he was determined to succeed.

He sat under the leadership of John Maxwell, a high-profile leader in the Christian world and a man whose expertise in leadership is much sought after. His time is valuable and expensive. But Sam spent money, time, and a great deal of effort to learn from someone who knew about leadership. He combined Maxwell's teaching with his own ideas and developed his own uniqueness.

Today, Dr. Samuel Chand gets calls from around the world. His vision is not just to train leaders but to train great leaders to make them even greater and more powerful in their influence in the world. In 2007, the website www.leadershipgurus.com asked members to vote on the thirty top leaders in the country. Sam Chand was number twenty-three. That's not bad for a man who didn't know if he could do it.

A major reason Dr. Chand stands where he does now is because he learned from someone who was more valuable—someone whose time he considered more valuable. John Maxwell is at the top of that leadership-guru list. Because he helped Dr. Chand (and certainly others) Dr. Maxwell is even more in demand. Many of those who are at the top in their fields have gone to Dr. Maxwell for his help. His minutes are more valuable because he can make others more valuable.

Don't overlook those seconds and minutes that pass by every day. The world can change just that fast. Just think: In one minute or less Jesus redeemed all of humanity so they would have a life, a purpose, and a destiny to fulfill. Earlier He prayed in the Garden of Gethsemane because He knew the suffering that lay ahead. He could have run away (and He certainly didn't want to suffer and die) but He made His decision. His 60-second decision is summed up in these words: "Nevertheless not My will, but Yours, be done" (Luke 22:42b).

Despite His inner turmoil, Jesus made that decision to say yes to God. By that single choice, salvation is available for all of us.

And there is more than salvation. He also offers you life that has meaning and gives you the opportunity to pass on the good things you have received. For example, Jesus told His disciples, and that includes you, "I am the door. If anyone enters by Me, he will be saved . . . I have come that they may have life, and that they may have *it* more abundantly" (John 10:9–10). That's just one more thing that came out of Jesus' 60-second decision in the Garden.

I'm a pastor of a large church on the east side of Atlanta. I love my congregation and I want to help people and want to do anything I can to help them live that abundant life Jesus promised. I have a dream—a vision—that I want to see fulfilled. When it's fulfilled it will empower everyone who participates. I want people to start thinking in new ways. I want to hear reports like this: "Sixteen months ago I stopped working for minimum wage because you helped me think differently. Nine months ago I opened my own business. Last week I made a sizeable down payment on my first house."

That's not impossible. In fact, that very message came to me in an e-mail from a member of our congregation. I know it's possible; I know because she has moved from the bottom rung and climbed way, way up the ladder of success.

I know it can happen—and it can happen to you.

Before you read any further, I want to make it clear that I'm against people working for minimum wage. There's no minimum wage when you're in the kingdom. If you maximize the value of each minute and accept the possibilities that lie in front of you, you'll never have to settle for getting by. Yes, many people never move beyond minimum wage, but that's because they have chosen to stay there.

You don't have to stay there. In America today, there is no excuse for bringing home the smallest paycheck. It may be the place you have to start; it shouldn't be the place you finish.

Too many people have no idea what Jesus meant when He said those words I quoted above: "I have come that they may have life, and that they may have *it* more abundantly" (John 10:10b). Abundant living isn't working for minimum wage. Abundant living isn't trying to figure out how to pay the rent and buy groceries with too small an income. Abundant living isn't being forced to ask others to give you a ride to church because you can't afford to buy a car.

When I dream of others living abundantly, I dream of seeing people who come behind me with genuine, authentic experiences. They are people who are serious about changing their lives and living in the abundance God promises. They don't have to become millionaires, although some do. What they have to do is to make that split-second decision that says, "I will change. I will not allow life to crush me."

I'm tired of folk playing religious church, regurgitating the same old words, ending up with a sorrowful face, and saying, "Bishop, pray for me." They want something or someone to help them and they come to me or the other ministers because they feel they need to be pepped up.

I'm not interested in pepping up people, but I am interested in seeing their lives changed. This isn't just a new idea that Bishop Eddie Long dreamed up and decided to preach.

I see the promises all through the Bible. The language may be different, but the intent is the same. For example, I point you to the prophet-priest named Ezra. He came along after the Persian king allowed Jews to return to Jerusalem. Ezra understood. He didn't depend on anything but God.

King Artaxerxes gave Ezra permission to return and rebuild Jerusalem. Along the way, Ezra made the people stop by the River Ahava for three days while they fasted and prayed. Here are Ezra's words: "Then I proclaimed a fast there at the river of Ahava, that we might humble ourselves before our God, to seek from Him the right way for us and our little ones and all our possessions. For I was ashamed to request of the king an escort of soldiers and horsemen to help us against the enemy on the road, because we had spoken to the king, saying, 'The hand of our God *is* upon all those for good who seek Him, but His power and His wrath *are* against all those who forsake Him'" (Ezra 8:21–22).

I hope you get that. Ezra wanted God to provide protection for their team and to lead them to Jerusalem. He refused to ask the king to take care of them. It's not the same as relying on the government to provide minimum wage, but the principle is the same: If you trust God, you can move beyond your poverty. If you turn to the government for help, you'll survive—barely. If you choose to use your gifts and build on your unique gifts just as Sam Chand did, you'll understand. You'll know that Jesus wants you to survive abundantly. You'll also know that He wants to help you do that.

After Ezra reached Jerusalem, he made all the people of Israel stand in an open square in the newly rebuilt city while he read the Law of Moses "from morning until midday, before the men and women and those who could understand; and the ears of all the people *were attentive* to the Book of the Law" (Nehemiah 8:3). The priests read the Law all day long "and they gave the sense, and helped *them* to understand the reading" (verse 8). After the reading of the Law, Ezra said, "The joy of the LORD is your strength" (verse 10).

He meant that God not only wanted them to hear what they were supposed to do (and the leaders explained so they would understand), they were to go out and obey. If they obeyed what they heard, God's joy would strengthen them. He meant that they would know who God was and they would know who they were. That knowledge would fill them with joy and gratitude and strengthen them as they moved ahead.

Not much has changed since the time of Ezra. Believers already have the strength available. The joy waits for people to catch the vision and to accept it. Those who catch the 60-second-change vision don't need to be pepped up. They won't find the joy from the world or from believing the lies they hear that they can't get any better or move upward in this life.

You can get better. Your life can get better. You can enter into the joy of the Lord and enjoy the life God wants you to have. Please read that again: *The life God wants you to have.*

If you start at the right place, you can end at the right place. I'll tell you exactly the right place to start. It begins with the question Jesus asked His disciples, "But who do you say that I am?" (Matthew 16:15).

"Simon Peter answered and said, 'You are the Christ, the Son of the living God'" (verse 16).

Like Peter, that's the first question you need to answer. Who is Jesus? Who is Jesus in your life? Before you try to figure out who you're going to marry, when you're going to go to school, where you're going to live, how much money you need, or when you're going to retire, this is the question for you to answer. Jesus isn't a great prophet like Elijah or just a good man. He's not in the god pool so you can call him out whenever you want. He is the only true and living God, all by Himself.

Peter's statement is more than just the correct answer. He knew that Jesus was the Christ—the Messiah—the Savior. He could answer the question correctly only because he had already had an encounter with God. Jesus said to him, "Blessed are you, Simon Bar-Jonah, for flesh and blood has not revealed *this* to you, but My Father who is in heaven" (verse 17).

I hope you understand that statement. People didn't tell Simon Peter who Jesus was. He didn't hear it as a Sunday school message. Peter didn't get it rubbed on him by the bishop. That insight came because Peter had met Jesus face-to-face and he believed.

There was more. Jesus went on to say to him, "And I also say to you that you are Peter, and on this rock I will build My church, and the gates of Hades shall not prevail against it" (verse 18). He says to Peter and to anyone else that on the rock of belief He builds His church.

It's as if Jesus said, "I build My church on your recognition of My identity." He refers to the church as the body of Christ. When you become a Christian, you become part of what we call the mystical body of Christ. He is the head, and you join with others throughout the ages who are His arms, feet, and voice.

And it's not just a message from Jesus or from the New Testament. Proverbs 22:29 reads, "Do you see a man who excels in his work? He will stand before kings; He will not stand before unknown men." *Unknown* means obscure and insignificant. He means that if you are diligent in your daily business life, you will be changed, and God will bless you so that you don't just show up in front of common, everyday people, you will show up before kings.

He means that when individuals work and do things well, they are brought into the presence of those with power. That applies to you as much as anyone else in the universe. If you are faithful to God, you can be assured that God will be faithful to you.

Here's an example. I had breakfast one morning with a Christian brother who is in his thirties. He knew who he was and knew what God could do in his life. He had grown up in an impoverished neighborhood with parents who struggled each month to pay the rent. However, that didn't hold back my friend. He believed he could achieve and he did.

"What are you doing next week?" I asked.

"I'm going to England."

"Really? A vacation?"

He shook his head and smiled. "I have an appointment to meet with the queen and then I'll—"

I didn't hear the rest of the sentence: I was too overawed. He was going to meet with the Queen of England. He was ready to meet royalty because he knew his life was grounded in Christ. He had made that 60-second turnaround when he was in his teens. That 60-second decision changed the direction of his life.

Your life can change, too. You can attain greatness with that simple 60-second decision.

60 SECONDS TO THINK

Try to imagine that you have just started to live your last day on earth. You know you will die tomorrow. Think about the questions below because the time will come when it truly is your last day on earth.

Take 60 seconds to answer each of these questions:

1. What are three ways in which my life mattered?

2. Who will remember me and what will they say about me?

3. What have been the three most important things in my life?

4. To what did I devote most of my time and my energy?

5. What greatness have I accomplished?

2

Personal Encounter with God

I want you to have a life plan and I want to help you make one that satisfies you and leads you to greatness in your life. Before you can do that, however, you need to have a personal, intimate encounter with God.

I'd like you to take one minute to make certain you have had a godly encounter. This isn't about going to church, serving in a soup kitchen, or singing a lot of hymns. This is about meeting Jesus Christ the Savior.

Before you go any further, I want you to have an encounter that will transform your life. It's not enough just to have your name written in heaven, but it's for you to be involved in an ongoing, daily intimacy with the Creator of your soul.

In many churches, we've emphasized church membership. Maybe we do that too much, especially by insisting people come forward and proclaim their sinfulness and their need for Jesus

Christ. Too often that practice has disintegrated into joining an organization and it doesn't always lead to an encounter with God. The gospel methods that worked with your grandparents don't necessarily work today.

Today's seekers think like this: If I like the church, if I like the programs, if I like how the preacher preaches, I'll go on the Internet and check out what they do and what kind of activities go on besides Sunday morning. Then I'll decide if I want to get involved.

That's the mentality. I'm not judging it; I'm only pointing out how it works. Eventually, many of them join New Birth (or any other church) based on what the church can do for them. Notice that: what the church can do for *them*.

"Why not?" a woman asked me. "Isn't that the way we choose schools for our children, especially when we consider college? We ask a lot of questions. Is it accredited? Does it have a good football team? Who are the teachers and are they good? What kind of credentials do they have? Is the school convenient to my home?"

That person was right about colleges but she was wrong about the church. At the door of the church is where the situation changes. Yes, the church serves, but those of us who come through those doors are also the servants. We focus on what we can do for each other inside our membership as well as what we can do for those who don't enter our doors.

What can you do to help? Who needs you? Those are good questions for you to ponder. If you do and put your thoughts into action, you'll also discover that in helping others, God helps you. In giving we receive, in helping we're helped.

The mind-set of modern seekers is one important reason megachurches grow: A bigger church usually means they have great leadership and also it means they can offer more to their parishioners. The variety of things going on around a megachurch can astound first-time visitors. For example, let's say a newcomer asks about a particular sport and someone on staff says, "Yes, we have athletic programs, such as soccer, football, racquetball, and basketball. We also offer aerobics and weight training."

"But what about spiritual help?"

They'll be quick to add, "We have counseling ministries with trained staff who can help with emotional, spiritual, or financial problems."

They see your teens with you and before you can catch your breath, you hear, "Yes, we have programs for youth. We offer job training, health fairs, and college assistance programs. We have several mentoring programs, men's programs, and women's programs."

While you're trying to absorb all the information, the person says, "If you have a need and don't see a program that meets it, let us know and we'll do what we can to start one."

That's how megachurches function. When people come along, we can plug them into a program that meets their needs and we're able to provide them with what they want. They are excellent programs. We have top-quality leaders.

But again I want to be clear: Even when people sign up for those programs, it doesn't mean they've made a decision to live right. It means they have gone where they found programs to meet their felt needs. That's not wrong; it's just not enough.

That kind of situation also makes it easy to church jump. If people are not heavily committed, little things can upset them and they will move on. It can be as minor as the traffic flow, too many people on the racquetball courts, the length of a sermon, or the "wrong kind" of music. If there's no commitment, there's no sense of feeling they have a divine destiny or purpose. So for many of the church hoppers it makes no difference which church they attend.

Let's try it the other way. Instead of looking at what the church or any group will do for you, what if you focused on having a change of heart? That change starts when you meet God on a personal level. That may be the moment when you know you're loved, and you commit yourself to follow Him. Many people make the head decision to come to church but they don't connect that with a heart decision. I want everyone to seek an encounter with God. But too often seekers come in as sinners and they go out as sinners.

I want to see hearts changed. This book is about change that starts on the inside and works its way outside and challenges your attitudes, your behaviors, and the way you live.

Because of wanting to see people's hearts change, for many years I followed the traditional method of preaching the best I could and ending with an invitation to come forward and surrender to Jesus Christ.

But something made me rethink that approach. I learned that although my intention was good and my heart was right, it didn't mean I always used the best methods. I wanted to keep learning how to be more effective in leading people to a heart-encounter with Jesus.

For instance, the first time I worshiped at Tony Evans's church he preached a wonderful message. Traditionally a preacher will finish a sermon with a killer statement and plead with people to come forward. Tony preached so powerfully I knew he would squeeze the congregation to get all those new converts to surge forward. I wanted to study his technique and see if I could learn something from him.

Instead, he said quietly, "I'm giving the benediction. If any of you have heard the voice of the Lord and want to follow Jesus Christ, there will be some folk standing up here and they'll take you in."

Just those simple words and he pronounced the benediction.

Tony, you missed an opportunity, I thought. I didn't understand what he did. He didn't push, urge, plead, or beg anyone to surrender their lives to Jesus. It was as if he said, "Okay, I've done my best and told you about Jesus Christ. If God has touched your heart and you truly want to have a personal encounter with Him, you can do that after we close the service. You can make your way up here while the rest of us go home."

He didn't make it slick or glamorous, and surely not emotional. He certainly didn't pull for people to weep and wail as they hurried forward. He didn't use that special music to whip it up to make people feel emotional so they would get out of their seats and come forward. Tony, I thought, you did everything wrong.

But as I pondered what he had done, I knew Tony Evans had done the right thing. Those who had been touched *would* find their way to the front. They didn't have to be begged. In fact, if we have to beg, isn't that forcing them? And as the old saying goes, "A man forced against his will is of the same opinion still."

If God had spoken to them, as Tony indicated, they wouldn't be able to sit still. If they had made that all-important, life-changing decision, they would have to take action of some kind. Tony gave them the *opportunity*, but they had to make their own decision.

As I pondered that day at Tony Evans's church, I asked if our approach had been wrong. Maybe we've tried to do the work of the Holy Spirit and bring conviction that only God can bring.

Since that day at Tony Evans's church, I've often ended the service the same way at New Birth Church. It's not easy for me to do that because I've been conditioned to nudge and to beg people. I've been giving altar calls for twenty-plus years. Many times I've thought if I don't invite them to confess to Jesus Christ, I'll lose somebody. They'll leave here without knowing Jesus Christ.

But another part of me says, "Yes, if you pull hard enough, they'll come forward, they'll pray and they'll say all the right words. But will their hearts be changed? Have their emotions been stirred but their hearts not converted?" I also wondered why they came forward. Was it because of an emotional moment or a painful situation when they were vulnerable? Was it truly the Holy Spirit who brought conviction? Did they just need a chance for emotional release and now they're free to go back to their old ways?

I also know that most churches have a back door, a very large back door, so that almost as many leave as those who come in. Many of those who pray, "I am a sinner," one Sunday can't be found a month later. Under the old system, we had folks join us one Sunday and we couldn't find them the next. They listed wrong addresses or inaccurate telephone numbers—as if they didn't want to be found. We've learned to discount 20 percent of the new ones who come forward at the end of the service. We know we won't see them again.

Maybe Tony Evans was right.

I have an order of worship but whenever God shows up my order is gone. Yet there is still order. There are times we experience an attitude of praise and worship that's phenomenal. At those times, I don't move fast trying to get to my sermon. Sometimes I don't even preach my sermon. Instead, I try to listen—really listen—and hear the Spirit of the Lord in that moment. God can speak to all His people and it doesn't have to be through preachers like me. And during those powerful moments, there is just as much of a direct, major encounter going on between God and the people who worship as there is between the Lord and me. At that moment, God doesn't need me to do anything except sit still and listen.

That's a problem some pastors have in this new kind of swing of events. They think God needs them and that God can't operate among the congregation without their leading it. When God shows up, sometimes He may want the leaders to shut up. He may be working on somebody in the balcony in a different way than He is working on someone in the front row or someone in the choir.

When the glory of the Lord is in the house and I stand up to talk or hurry into my message, I interrupt God at work. If I move or say anything, I'll disrupt the Holy Spirit's work, so I'm learning how to be patient. I'm learning to read God. If it means people will come, grow, and lie down before the altar, I'm not going to disturb that. I didn't ask them to come forward, but apparently the Holy Spirit did.

One thing that deeply touches me is to see teenagers weeping, praying, and crying out for God to forgive them. When that happens spontaneously, that's not manipulation. They rush forward without being pulled, enticed, or begged. That is an authentic move of God and when I'm at church I'm going to let the Lord have His way.

I try to be open to talk when God wants me to speak. I have to hear God say, "Open your mouth." The proof to me that I did the right thing shows because of the great testimonies throughout the week from members of the congregation by e-mail.

Previously, we rarely received any immediate responses from the congregation, but the Internet has changed that. People from all over the world now send e-mail messages. It says they're watching and they let us know their responses and allow us to rejoice with them after they have made significant decisions.

It's phenomenal and we have to be able to shift to meet people where they are. They're into real-world stuff and they want to come to a church where they sense they can feel good because they've been accepted.

People aren't stupid. They know when we do something mechanical or purely from ritual. They also sense it when God intervenes and touches their hearts.

When I talk about this, inside my head I carry a picture of the concept I want to share. I study all week and I can "see" what I want to communicate. My picture is twenty inches by twenty. I describe it the best I can but when I do, it may become only ten inches by ten to those who hear it. Still it's the best I can do.

I have to stretch myself to project a big picture to those who listen and stretch in such a way that they can grasp what the Spirit is saying behind the words.

The responsibility belongs to those who hear what I say. If I teach or preach the best I can, I've done what I need to do. At least seven times in the book of Revelation it lays the burden on those who hear. So if God does that in the Bible, should I do less? "He who has an ear, let him hear what the Spirit says to the churches" (see Revelation 2:7, 11, 17, 29; 3:6, 13, 22; and see also 13:9).

I know there's a big difference between hearing and truly hearing. Someone put it this way, "She hears me, but she doesn't listen to anything I say." I understand and it reminds me of when I was a kid. My daddy would tell me to empty the trash and I'd nod or say, "Yeah, okay," but I didn't get moving. I stayed in front of the TV and watched cartoons.

A few minutes later, Daddy would say, "Did you hear me?"

The second time, his voice was louder and I knew I had to do something. I had heard his words the first time, but the second time I heard the words as a call to action that meant, "Do it now." I got up fast and emptied the trash.

The point I want to make is that the proof of hearing—real hearing—results in doing. I expect members of my congregation to be extremely prayerful. I don't want them to come to Sunday worship for their Bible study; I want them to have Bible study every day. I want them to read the Bible and pray every day. If they do that, by the time I minister to them, I don't have to give them a fresh revelation. Instead, I actually give them confirmation.

And most times I can tell who's really with me when I pull out my Bible and I say, "Let's turn to Mark 15." People start to say, "Wow," or "Yes," and say it with enthusiasm because they know that passage. Some will have studied it just that week. They have had no conversation with me but during that week they were drawn to Mark 15, or they have discussed that chapter with someone. I confirm and fill in the blanks of something they're already doing.

I don't want them to come to church expecting this man or that woman to be a giant spiritual guru while they sit like blank slates waiting for somebody to write words on their hearts. I want them to have their own devotional life where they're "prayed up," so that when someone stands up to speak, they are already fully in the conversation. And what is marvelous about all that is I haven't talked directly to any of them.

But evidently we've all talked to the same Man. And the beauty of it is that they'll have studied Mark or some text and what I say adds to their understanding and supports what they've been studying. As I speak and confirm, the Bible opens up for them. When that happens, they're not looking at my ten-by-ten picture but they can see the twenty-by-twenty for themselves. We're looking at the same picture.

I don't want you to be lazy Christians. I don't want you to be able to say, "It's true because Bishop Long said it." I want you to say, "It's true because it's in the Bible and I also know it's true because I've experienced it in my heart." I want you to be able to say, "This is what I know. This is what I've experienced."

When you talk that way, I know you've made that 60-second decision to follow Jesus Christ. Your words and your attitude are proof of your encounter with God and tell me that you're on the road to greatness. You're not getting a secondhand testimony because I've worked through what I preach. You hear my words and you shout about something you know firsthand.

When I speak I want you to be like the people of Berea. In the book of Acts, Paul and Silas preached at the city of Thessalonica, but the people were so hostile the preachers were forced to leave. Immediately they went to the city of Berea. "When they arrived, they went into the synagogue of the Jews. These were more fair-minded than those in Thessalonica in that they received the word with all readiness, and searched the Scriptures daily to find out whether these things were so" (Acts 17:10–11).

When I refer to the Berean account, I mean that I want every saint—everyone who comes into the presence of the Lord, including you—to come into a mighty experience in worship so often that they are like bottles with a cork in them. And they will come in after having been dipped in the anointing and the full flow of God's Spirit.

I'll explain that. Did you ever notice what happens when you take an empty bottle with a cork in it and plunge it into the water? Almost immediately, the bottle becomes wet on the outside, and as soon as you take it out of the water and hold it up, the water starts to drip off. The bottle soon becomes dry. But when you pull out that cork and stick the bottle back into the water and dip it all the way under, it gets filled with water.

That's the experience I want for people when they come to church and into the presence of other believers. I want them to be like the bottle with the cork that's been popped. The presence of the Lord doesn't just touch us and move around us, but fills us inside where it won't run out.

60 SECONDS TO THINK

I want you to take this personal journey with me and with other readers of this book. But you have to start at the right place. I don't care if you're a fifty-year church member or have only attended church five times in your life. You still have to start at the right place—at the beginning.

I want you to examine yourself for one full minute. After you've done that, I want you to choose which one of the sentences below applies to you:

1. I am a believer and have faithfully followed Jesus Christ.

2. I am a believer and I've tried to follow Jesus Christ, and I do it most of the time.

3. I'm a believer but I've failed God more often than I've obeyed, but I truly want to be obedient to God.

4. I'd like to believe so I can follow Jesus Christ.

After you have selected the sentence that best describes you, write the answers to the following questions:

- What is one *decision* I must make to prove to myself and to others that I want to follow Jesus Christ?

- What one *action* do I need to take to prove to myself and to others that I want to follow Jesus Christ?

Write these words: "I will." This is your way of saying to yourself and to God that you are willing to do whatever God asks of you.

3

Get Out of the Boat

Jesus said one word to Peter, "Come."

It's in a powerful story about waves tossing the boat around on the Sea of Galilee. In the middle of the night Jesus appeared to the frightened disciples and He was walking on the sea. They cried out in fear, but Jesus spoke to them and told them not to be afraid. That seemed to calm them.

Peter, always the bold one, yelled out, "Lord, if it is You, command me to come to You on the water" (Matthew 14:28b).

That's when Jesus called out, "Come."

"And when Peter had come down out of the boat, he walked on the water to go to Jesus." Matthew 14:22–33 contains the story of Peter walking on the water—if only for a short distance. "But when [Peter] saw that the wind was boisterous, he was afraid; and beginning to sink he cried out, saying, 'Lord, save me!' And immediately Jesus stretched out His hand and caught him . . ."

We can smirk about Peter because he became afraid and began to sink but instead, we need to clap for him: He believed. He got out of the boat. He was the only disciple who did.

So I have a message for you: Be like Peter. Get out of the boat!

You'll never make the right choices as long as you shudder and stay safe inside the boat. Get out. Take a risk. Trust Jesus' strong arms to grab you if you begin to fall.

In the previous chapter, I asked you to write "I will." Now I warn you: If you say or write, "I will," you have to do what Peter did. He left the others who were too afraid to move and wouldn't get out of the boat. If you're going to walk with Jesus, you have to get away from the crowd. Of course, there will always be people— maybe your own family members—who will call you crazy. "Nobody can walk on water. You fool."

Don't listen to their expressions of shortsightedness. Don't be so tied to them that you miss Jesus while He walks past you on the water.

Or if you don't like the picture of walking on the water, you can answer all your critics by saying, "I'm following the example of the prophet Habakkuk. He got away from the crowd by standing, waiting, and watching. The prophet wrote to the confused and disobedient people of Israel: 'I will stand my watch And set myself on the rampart, And watch to see what He will say to me ...'" (Habakkuk 2:1). When you do that, when you climb up into the watchtower, wait. Wait and listen; God will speak. When you come down, you can say, "I heard God tell me what to do."

Whether you follow Peter or Habakkuk, you won't hear God speak until you do *something*. Some of you are still inside the boat. You want to get out but your friends tell you that you can't do it.

You'd like to have a business but they remind you that 80 percent of businesses fail the first year. You'd like to change jobs, but they remind you that you have security where you are, even if the pay isn't very good. You'd like to move but they remind you how many companies have foreclosed on mortgages. There are always voices that cry, "Don't get out of the boat! Stay here with us."

Don't listen to them. Listen to Peter: "Command me to come to You on the water."

Or you can follow the words of the Old Testament prophet and move away from the negative voices. Refuse to let them tear you down and discourage you. Listen again to the words of Habakkuk: "I will watch to see what He will say to me." He listened. He heard directly from God and wrote in Habakkuk 2:20, "But the LORD is in His holy temple. Let all the earth keep silence before Him."

He meant, "The Lord is closer than you think." He is prepared to listen, but they had to be prepared to wait and to hear. The prophet knew that and he could shout, "I will stand." He was determined to get himself in the right place and continue to listen to God. "I'm going to station myself in that spot and I won't move. I'll offer myself to God and I'll continue to wait as long as it takes."

Habakkuk climbed into a tower—a solid place—and a place away from everyone else, and especially away from those whose negative voices tried to pull him down. It's like standing on a rock: and that solid, unmovable rock is Christ Jesus and it's also the Word of God. He is a strong tower. "I'll get into the tower, I'll stand on Christ; I'll stand on the Word and I won't give in."

But the prophet didn't just stand there. That was only the first part of his plan: He climbed into the tower and stood there *for a purpose.* He went alone into that solid, strong chamber to wait for

God to speak His messages to us. If they were written in modern words, they would read like this: "I wait and will continue to wait and to be on watch until I receive the word I need. I'll lean forward and look into the future."

Too many people don't understand what it means to lean forward. They want to lean backward. They want to tie themselves to their past because it's easier and safer than to take a risk. They failed in the past, so obviously they'll fail in the future. They didn't finish high school or college. They lack skills and can't get a better job. They don't try to improve their skills or get better jobs. They're leaning backward. "That's the way it used to be," they say to themselves. "That's the way it is. That's how it will always be."

Wrong! That's how it *was*. Your future can be different!

Lean forward. Take action. Get out of the boat! Walk on the water! Climb into the tower! Instead of feeling sorry for yourself, you need to be on your tiptoes, peering into the future to see what God has for you.

Read these two words aloud: "I will."

That's where the future starts. If you can't get excited about your tomorrow, nobody can get excited for you. A lot of people won't get excited for you and will even try to put out the fire of your enthusiasm. Don't listen to them. You may have to stand alone in that high tower, but that's where God speaks. That's where God's plan can become a reality for you.

"I will."

God spoke to the frustrated and confused prophet and told him to write his vision (see Habakkuk 2:2). He told him to write the words on a tablet and to write them so large that even if someone were running and was still a long way off, that person could read the words. "Write your vision."

"I will."

But what is it you will? Is it your dream of a great future for yourself or is it God's will? You have to learn to separate what you want from what God wants for you.

I want to add this as comfort to you: No matter what you want, God always wants the best for you and it's often greater than you had expected. So if you listen for His voice and follow His directions, you'll always have the best He has planned for you.

It's not always easy to surrender what you want. If you're like most people, you have definite ideas and sometimes it takes a lot of surrendering before you're ready to let God direct you.

When Jesus prayed in the Garden of Gethsemane, He didn't want to die. "O My Father, if it is possible, let this cup pass from Me; nevertheless, not as I will, but as You will" (Matthew 26:39b). Matthew tells us He prayed that way two times. It may have been twice or it may have been a way to say that He cried out alone in the Garden for a long time. That was the perfect human being; that was the sinless One, and even He struggled.

Jesus cried out for God to show Him an easier way. He was a human being and He didn't want the physical pain and torture that He knew would be His immediate future. Who would have wanted that? I'm sure Jesus would have preferred a nice, comfortable, and predictable life as a carpenter in Nazareth. But He knew God's plan for Him and after much agonized prayer, Jesus was able to cry out, "O My Father, if this cup cannot pass away from Me unless I drink it, Your will be done" (verse 26:42).

Six hundred years earlier, Habakkuk understood that principle. If he wanted the best, if he wanted God's favor, he had to let go of his own way and give himself totally to God.

God speaks and, in effect, says to the prophet, "Get yourself to a place where you can be alone with Me and you won't have other voices filling your head. Go there and I'll speak to you and tell you what I've created you for. Spend the time to write it and make it plain to the people who will read your words. Engrave the message into your mind and your heart."

If writing was good enough for Habakkuk, isn't it good enough for you today?

Before you read any further, go to the end of this chapter and write these words: "I will get out of the boat." Your boat won't be someone else's boat. You need to find what keeps you inside, and what makes you afraid and unable to get up and move forward.

Make that 60-second decision and write that simple sentence.

Get out of the boat!

If you start with those words and follow through with them, you can write the rest of the things that I'll show you. You can write the words for the next generation. You can start walking down the right path and the next generation will be ready to follow. Once you discover who God made you to be, Habakkuk says you can run with the message.

In those days with no form of mass communication, they sent messengers on foot from one place to another. They used fast, sure-footed men. Those special runners received the message and ran as fast as they could to deliver it. Think of yourself as being one of those fast, sure-footed messengers. And you are. You are God's messenger in the present time. Your job is to deliver the word your heart hears when you're alone in the solitary place. If you hear the message of God's will correctly, you'll know and you'll be ready for action. After you hear, you can run swiftly forward because you will have the word for the next generation. They will follow you as you follow the right path.

Not only are you a messenger, but one way or another you will carry a message to the next generation. You carry the message right now—today—by the way you conduct your life, by the way you behave around others, the places you go, and the way you treat other people. If you're faithful, you'll carry the correct message. If you don't wait to hear from God, you'll deliver the wrong one and you may lead others astray or confuse them.

If you're faithful to God, the next generation won't ask you what you're about—they won't have to ask. They'll see and they'll know you speak the truth because you live the truth in your day-to-day tasks. And they'll join you if you're connected to God. They'll know if you've heard and are running with the message. They'll also know if you're not connected. They may not know everything about God, but they do know the difference between the real and the fake.

It's amazing but many, many unsaved people know who runs with the right message, even if they don't follow them. A drunk on the street who's not saved will sit up and holler at you, "Hey, woman of God." How does he know? Somehow people sense the presence of God in your life.

My cowriter, Cecil Murphey, was once involved in a national men's organization. He had been with the organization about two years when a man named Henry called. Henry wasn't a member of the men's group; he had attended once but didn't stick around. He had just broken up with his girlfriend. He was so distraught, he felt like killing himself. Before he did, however, he called Cec. His first words were, "I'm desperate. I need your help or I'm going to take my own life."

After they talked for a long time, Henry calmed down. He said he felt better. He even talked about God (and later became a believer). Before the conversation ended, Cec asked Henry why he had called him. "You don't know me all that well. There are others—"

"But you're a Christian and a man of God," Henry said.

Cec is a full-time writer, but he's also an ordained minister. However, this wasn't something Cec spoke openly about at the men's group.

"How do you know that?" Cec asked. "I've never said anything publicly."

Henry laughed. "Everyone knows who you are."

That's how it works, isn't it? You may think no one knows, but the reality is that almost everyone knows you or at least knows a lot about you. They know by the way you run with the message. They can tell by the way you walk down the street that you've got a clear picture of who you are, they know you by the way you talk or the tone of your voice. They know who you are by the movies you attend and those you won't attend. There is certain music you won't listen to. If you're running with the true message, it causes you to go and get certain books and read and study because you're constantly filling yourself with the direction that you're going. Day by day you're becoming more sure where you're going and your purpose shows. So what you are right now is a small picture of who you will eventually become.

Many may have the vision but they don't "become" the vision. Many people have not become their vision. That is, they know what God says on the rampart but they won't allow it to grow inside and change them.

It's not enough to think about it. You have to do something.

I will. Remember?

60 SECONDS TO THINK

1. Write these words: "I will get out of the boat." This is your commitment to yourself and to God that you will take action. You will form a plan. This is your way to say that regardless of the storms around you, you will overcome the fear and ignore the negative voices. *You will get out of the boat.*

2. List the things that could stop you from getting out of the boat. It may be your fear, your uncertainty, or your lack of education. It may be lack of encouragement from anyone. It may involve circumstances in your life, a lack of self-confidence that you can change. It may be that you don't think you're good enough, smart enough, old enough, or young enough. Write down each of those hindrances.

3. After you have written each of those things, write after each one: "I will get out of the boat." That is your way of saying, "I won't be held prisoner to anything that holds me back or tries to enslave me." You may have to ask others to help, but determine to get out of the boat and walk on the waves.

4. Write this sentence: "If I get out of the boat, Jesus won't let me sink." Read your statements above about the hindrances, and your statement that you will get out of the boat. Now add this one: "If I get out of the boat, Jesus won't let me sink." For example: "I'm too weak to stay with my commitment, but I will get out of the boat. If I get out of the boat, Jesus won't let me sink."

4

60 SECONDS FOR A

Vision

In Habakkuk 2:1–4, the prophet writes about his vision: "I will stand my watch And set myself on the rampart, And watch to see what He will say to me, And what I will answer when I am corrected. Then the LORD answered me and said: 'Write the vision And make *it* plain on tablets, That he may run who reads it. For the vision *is* yet for an appointed time; But at the end it will speak, and it will not lie. Though it tarries, wait for it; Because it will surely come, It will not tarry.'"

I quote these four verses because I want to emphasize five things God says about the vision:

1. It is for an appointed time.

2. It will speak.

3. It will not lie.

4. It will surely come.

5. It will not tarry (won't be delayed).

1. It is for an appointed time.

As you read these statements, I want you to get excited about what God has in store for you. You have a purpose to fulfill on this earth. You have a destiny. Only as you open yourself to the vision will you be able to understand your purpose and your destiny.

"Really?" you may ask with skepticism. "Who me? Who am I?"

You are God's creation, that's who. More than that, you do have a purpose and a destiny. That's true, even if you don't believe it. It's true even if you're unsure, doubtful, or convinced that you don't matter. You do matter.

Many of you have heard it said that you are one of the people for whom Jesus died. That's true, but it's more than just that you're a surefire candidate for heaven. You are important to God's plan for the world. You have a role that only you can fulfill.

I think of the words of Mordecai to Queen Esther, "Who knows if perhaps you were made queen for such a time as this?" (Esther 4:14b, NLT). The wise man of God knew it was no accident that a Jewish woman had become Queen of Persia. She was there for a purpose—a divine purpose.

In case you don't know the story, Esther was a Jewish young woman, a nobody, but she found favor with the King of Persia, who sought a new wife. And because she followed her destiny—the plan

God had for her—Esther saved the Jewish people from extinction in Persia. One person did it, and she was a woman at a time when men had all the power.

Your role probably won't be to save a nation or to make drastic changes in the culture of your world. You may never be famous or have a street in your hometown named after you. Regardless of how small your role may seem, you have a function, a task, and like Esther, only you can fulfill that job.

No one in history may ever know what you've done. You may not even be a footnote in a history book. But your name will be written in large letters in God's records.

Do you know the name of the boy who brought his lunch to Andrew, and Jesus used it to feed five thousand? Do you know the name of the lame man healed by James and John in Acts chapter 3? Do you know the name of the soldier at the cross who cried out, "Truly this was the Son of God!" (Matthew 27:54). The answer is that none of those individuals are named. They were the seemingly insignificant people in the world, but God knows their names. And God had a purpose for each of them. The Bible is filled with people who did simple things such as share a lunch or speak up for God.

You can do the same. You will do the same if you catch the vision. The vision is a message for you: It is your destiny and your purpose in life. You may never be fully aware of your impact, but you'll never know anything about your destiny until you catch the vision.

I want you to catch the vision. I want you to take 60 seconds to grasp that important vision, the one intended for no one else in the world or in history except you. Don't waste your minutes. Every moment that ticks away is important. It is important for you. The ticking moments are also important for the next generation because you will make it easier or harder for them to follow.

Like Mordecai, I challenge you with these words: "Who knows if perhaps you were made queen for just such a time as this?"

God placed Esther on the throne at that appointed time—the time He appointed for her. The first thing the prophet said to the people was that his message was for an appointed time. "Write the vision And make *it* plain on tablets, That he may run who reads it. For the vision *is* yet for an appointed time . . ." (Habakkuk 2:2–3a).

The vision God offers you isn't one of those deals where you can choose to grab on to it anytime you please. Now is the time. Once you grab the vision, once you determine to do whatever God wants you to do in your life, you'll have fulfilled the first part: You'll have said yes during the appointed time.

I realize that when I write "the appointed time," I may confuse many readers. That's not my purpose. Yet though it is confusing, please think about this concept. Perhaps this illustration will help: When I was in third grade, our class put on a play based on the famous fairy tale *Hansel and Gretel*. I'm not sure why, but the teacher chose me to play the role of Hansel—the male star of the play. The play was for an "appointed time"—that is, a time when we would present it to the rest of the school and to our parents.

I thought I'd make an excellent Hansel and I liked being the hero of the story. I had been chosen for that role and it was, in one sense, my destiny. But it didn't work out that way.

I failed to fulfill my destiny. I failed to perform at the appointed time. I failed because I didn't memorize my lines. I intended to do that, but I kept putting it off and putting it off. As it turned out, someone else stepped in for the appointed time. I played the non-speaking role of the gingerbread man. I never got another chance to play Hansel.

Perhaps it will help if you look at life as if it's a play. Every actor is important. The success of the production depends on every person. If one person doesn't memorize the lines, someone else has to jump in, and it will be someone not intended for that role, but someone who has to cover up because you failed.

When you're onstage you're just as important as the lead actor or lead actress, even if your part is small. There's a famous show business saying, "There are no small roles; there are only small actors." It means every role is important and that includes everyone from the person who opens a door or the one who says one line all the way to the leading roles.

A play's success often depends on the timing. And if you're in a play, for you to fill your appointed time and your destiny, you have to be in the timing. You work with the others, and you put yourself where you belong, and you do everything you can to make it an excellent production.

God has put you in this life and at this time for a purpose that is made just for you. You are one of those chosen actors on life's stage. You are so important that at the appointed time—your lifetime—God created you and ordained you. You may never become the king or the queen, you may never be the lead actor on a grand stage, but you have an appointed part. When you hit the scene, when you accept your kingdom assignment, it is so important that, as far as God is concerned, you are the star of that moment. At that moment (and it may be for a brief time) you are the one who carries the message. Or I could say it this way: You are the one who carries the blessing or carries the word for that moment. Your appointed time makes you the lead actor.

When I speak about this at church, I sometimes hear from discouraged or depressed people. They've done what I told them. They've gotten out of the boat. They groan, "Bishop Long, I will. I will! I will! I got out of the boat. I've worked through everything on my list." They look sorrowfully at me and say, "But nothing has happened. Nothing has changed."

Part of getting out of the boat and of climbing onto the rampart is to wait. Wait. Wait and God will speak. That is, you will know what God wants you to do.

It might help to think of the story of Joseph in the Old Testament. When he was a boy, he had dreams in which God told him that he would rule over his older brothers and his father. They laughed at him; his father told him to stop talking that way. Yet Joseph knew.

What he didn't know was that it wasn't going to happen immediately. I don't know how old he was when he had his first dreams, but the Bible tells us he was seventeen years old when his brothers sold him into slavery to some traders on their way to Egypt.

How long did Joseph wait until he stood in power behind only Pharaoh? The answer is thirteen years. Or what about Abraham, the great father of the faith? He prayed for a son and when he was seventy-five years old, God promised he would have a son. He waited *twenty-five years for that promised son.*

So you're out of the boat. Now you wait.

2. It will speak.

You need to follow what I call the God Principle. I want to give you two examples.

First, God took seven days to create the world. Every day He did something. And He left a lot of things still undone. But what He did each day was good. If you read the creation story, at the end of each day God speaks about what He had done.

On the first day He created light and darkness or day and night. "And God saw the light, that it was good" (Genesis 1:4) and the Bible adds, "So the evening and the morning were the first day" (verse 5). Each day He did a little more. When He finished, He looked at His work, declared it good, and said it was the end of the day.

There was still some mess undone. But He looked at what He had accomplished, patted Himself on the back, and said, "It's good. Even though My seven-day program, My seven-day vision, is not complete on day two, I won't worry about what hasn't been done. I'll celebrate what has been accomplished. So when I wake up the next day I'll celebrate, knowing I've gotten two days out of the way. Today's the third day and I'm going to accomplish something on this third day. And I'm going to celebrate what I did at the end of the day."

That's how God works. Here's a second example: God led the Israelites out of Egypt. He told them to collect gold and silver from the Egyptians so they would have money. He told them to kill a lamb for every household and to eat the Passover meal in the middle of the night. They did those things in haste before they left Egypt. God took them forward and when they reached the Red Sea they realized that the Egyptians were pursuing them. But God was already preparing the next phase. He was already taking care of His people. God first put a cloud between the Egyptians and the Israelites. "And the Angel of God, who went before the camp of Israel, moved and went behind them; and the pillar of cloud went from before them and stood behind them . . . Thus it was a cloud and darkness to the [Egyptians] and it gave light by night to [Israel], so that the [Egyptians] did not come near the [Israelites] all that night" (Exodus 14:19, 20).

God didn't do everything at one time. The biblical account goes on and tells us the second thing: "Then Moses stretched out his hand over the sea; and the LORD caused the sea to go *back* by a strong east wind all that night, and made the sea into dry *land* . . ." (verse 21).

That's the God Principle. God seldom does everything in one great, continuous motion. There are steps along the way to make it happen.

3. It will not lie.

One of my favorite stories in the Old Testament is about a prophet named Balaam. He seems to be a kind of prophet who predicted good or bad things according to the amount of money received from whoever hired him. Balak, the King of the Moabites, hired Balaam to curse the Israelites. He tried but he couldn't do it. Balak paid him to try again and here's what he said to Balak and the Moabites: "God is not a man, that He should lie; Nor a son of man, that He should repent. Has He said, and will He not do? Or has He spoken, and will He not make it good? Behold, I have received a command to bless [a command from God]; He has blessed and I cannot reverse it" (Numbers 23:19–20).

I just want to caution you at this moment that so many things have been missed because you and I have made God to be less than what He is. And God will not lie; God will not deceive; God will not promise something He is unwilling to give. I repeat that because it's so important. God has never lied; God will not lie; God cannot lie; He has not lied and He will remain faithful even when you are not faithful. If God promises, wait because God speaks only truth. Don't miss out on receiving the fulfillment of the promises and the depth that God has for your life because you try to treat His promises as you would treat those of a human being.

It is remarkable how difficult it is for you and me to allow God to be God. I find myself reading Scripture and saying, "I have faith and I believe." But as I say those words, I still see God in my own image. That is, sometimes I fail and don't accomplish the things that I say I will. I promise to do something but I don't always carry it out. It's natural to think God operates the same way by making promises that might not be fulfilled.

I'm not the only one guilty of thinking that way (although none of us would say it out loud). Here's how I see it. We make God in our own image because we have been deceived or misled by so many people so often that even when we hear that He will not lie, it is hard for us to receive it. It's not easy to believe and hold on to the promise and to wait for the fulfillment. That's especially true if we have to wait.

Receiving such words with the natural or carnal mind means we cannot understand or discern the things of the Spirit. The apostle Paul says it this way: "These things we also speak, not in words which man's wisdom teaches but which the Holy Spirit teaches, comparing spiritual things with spiritual. But the natural man does not receive the things of the Spirit of God, for they are foolishness to him, nor can he know them, because they are spiritually discerned" (1 Corinthians 2:13–14).

We have missed so many wonderful things in God because we made God a man. He's not a human being that He should mislead us or hold back what He has promised. He will deliver. We sometimes struggle on that one because sometimes when we look at God, even though we see Him as the Almighty, we devalue Him and don't trust Him to the point that we know—know with total certainty—that He will bring to pass what He has promised.

4. It will surely come.

It will surely come. Isn't it amazing? We first say He won't lie and then we believe it will surely come.

I'll never forget when my wife and I were expecting our son, Jared. As I write these words, I have to say that I'm glad I'm a man. I don't think I could go through the process of carrying a baby and going through all the emotional and physical and spiritual things that women have to go through.

We knew we were going to have a child and we talked about it a lot. We didn't do anything, but we talked. Maybe two weeks before our baby was due we got really into the nesting stage. Knowing that the baby would surely come, we went into frenzied activities, such as getting a room ready for the baby. We bought a crib. People gave us diapers and we bought a lot more. By then, we knew the baby was going to be a boy, so we bought "boy" clothes and a lot of blue. As an expectant, proud father, I bought a few baseball and basketball toys he'd have to grow into. But the point I want to make is that we knew we were going to have a baby boy and we knew it would happen within the next two weeks. We did everything we could to get ready. In everything we did, we acted as if we expected the baby to come.

Jared arrived right on schedule.

When the Lord says, "It will surely come," it's even more certain than the birth of a child. And just as when anticipating the birth of a child, you do not sit, talk, and wait to see if it will happen. You get busy. You want to be ready.

Apply that idea to the promises of God. I challenge you to make preparations for the coming of the promises, for the fulfillment of what God wants to do in your life. Get yourself ready. Make the proper moves that show you're prepared.

By contrast, Jesus told a wonderful story about ten young women who were part of a wedding party. The main characters in the parable are ten maidens who await the arrival of the bridegroom. All ten carried lamps because the festivities were to take place at night. But the groom didn't come as soon as they expected. Because he delayed his arrival, the young women grew tired and went to sleep. At midnight, however, they were awakened by the news that the groom was on the way.

Little oil was left in their lamps after the long wait. That wasn't a problem for five of them because they had wisely brought along extra oil. The other five had been foolish; they had neither expected nor prepared for a delay. They didn't have enough oil.

The five who had prepared had only enough for themselves. They urged the others to hurry out and buy more. Even though it was midnight, it was possible that most of the villagers were outside waiting for the wedding celebration. Apparently they assumed that some merchant might sell them oil.

By the time those foolish women returned from buying oil, the groom had already arrived, collected the five bridesmaids, and was gone. He and his procession had entered into the marriage feast. When the five foolish women got there, they realized that the door to the feast was closed. The groom refused to let the latecomers inside.

Jesus interpreted His own parable (Matthew 25:1–13) and advised His followers to watch because they couldn't know the time of His return. He pleads with you and with me to be always prepared because it will surely come ("the Son of Man is coming").

What God promises will come. If you hold to that and remember, the promises build such wonderful excitement that they keep you encouraged and faithful as you go through the hard times. You keep on and remain faithful because you know, *you truly expect*, the blessed fulfillment of the promises of God in your life.

5. It will not tarry (won't be delayed).

One of my favorite Bible verses about God not tarrying is something written by the apostle Paul. I also write this as part of my personal testimony. Galatians 6:9 says, "And let us not grow weary while doing good, for in due season we shall reap if we do not lose heart." *The Message* says it like this: "So let's not allow ourselves to get fatigued doing good. At the right time we will harvest a good crop if we don't give up, or quit."

That's the blessing we want: Whenever God is ready to release something He releases it very quickly, but He may wait a long time before the release date. The promise of God will not wait or tarry beyond its due season. When God is ready, it happens and nothing can stop it.

One of the ways God tests your faith and your faithfulness is that He doesn't fulfill many promises immediately. And, as Paul implies, before the "due season," most of us grow tired. We wait and we're tired of waiting. We want it now, but God doesn't promise to deliver when we want it.

The promise of God is that you will reap if you don't quit. No one can know the exact date of harvest. But harvest season always comes. You can't always know when God is ready to fulfill the promises, but they won't tarry one day—not one moment—beyond God's time.

Years ago I read about the famous Welsh Revival that took place in 1904. The one thing I remember most was that Evan Roberts and others prayed fervently and faithfully for God to break through and revive the country of Wales. One part of that account has stayed with me through the years. A small group prayed faithfully and one of them quoted 2 Chronicles 7:14: "If My people who are called by My name will humble themselves, and pray and seek My face, and turn from their wicked ways, then I will hear from heaven, and will forgive their sin and heal their land."

They held on to that promise and obeyed the command to humble themselves and repent and God's reviving Spirit swept across the land. Those men prevailed in prayer. They obeyed the words of Paul: They didn't give up and so they reaped the harvest.

For most people, and you may be one of them, when it's getting close to the time for the promise of God, you're ready to give up. But when you feel like fainting, don't collapse. Instead, stand up, look around, and cry out to God to give you strength. Ask Him to help you prevail.

I want to tell you something about New Birth Missionary Church. I wanted to pastor a church and I knew God had called me to pastor a big church. It wasn't because of my ego or that I felt I had to have a big congregation, I simply knew that *big* was the adjective. As I waited and prayed, I knew, I absolutely knew, it was going to be a large congregation. Large to me was fifteen hundred members.

I prayed and I waited for God and I also witnessed God's promise fulfilled. When God was ready to pour out His blessings, things happened. When it was God's time, the church grew suddenly. It didn't wait. People started showing up. Sometimes forty new people came on a single Sunday. The next week it might be fifty, seventy, a hundred, or even two hundred. People came to Jesus Christ. They joined our church; and still more people kept coming to New Birth.

When we hit ten thousand members I was nearly worn out and wanted to faint, but as God had started it, God continued to make it happen. The church grew faster than I could get ready for it. Suddenly we hit twenty thousand members and the church kept on growing. We've now passed twenty-five thousand and we're right about thirty thousand folks. God did it a whole other way than how I thought it would happen. The growth came about so fast, I still thought and acted as if I was the senior pastor of a fifteen-hundred-member church.

One day a member said to me, "You are so blessed you didn't even realize it. He's already done it for you."

His words shocked me but as I reflected on what he said, I knew he was right: I had been so busy planning for fifteen hundred that God passed me by and kept it going so that I hardly knew what happened. And I have no idea where it will end. It won't end at our church facility in Lithonia, Georgia. We've already expanded around the world, and God is still shouting, "It won't be delayed."

In your life, it will happen; maybe it already has happened. Please be mindful of the prophet Isaiah's words: "Do not remember the former things. Nor consider the things of old. Behold, I will do a new thing. Now it shall spring forth; Shall you not know it?" (Isaiah 43:18–19).

It's amazing, because through the fast expansion of our church, I learned to hold on and wait. This much I know: When God starts to perform what He promised to do, it will take place. I figured out how New Birth would grow and I had a lot of ideas and plans. I've learned that we can make our plans, but God determines how they will turn out. Some wise person once said, "Man proposes; God disposes." That means that no matter how much we plan for God to work in a particular way, it won't happen *unless* that's the way God wants to operate.

While I kept trying to figure out patterns for God, I realized that He had already done many things in marvelous ways, so marvelous they were beyond my thinking. I kept figuring out how God would walk through the front door and He came in the back door. A few times I focused on the window and He came in through the front door. This means we need to pray for God to work, but we don't need to give Him instructions on how to do His job. He's too smart to listen to us anyway. The how—that is, the delivery system—that's totally in God's hands.

I want to add this warning: Don't tell God how to work. It won't do any good anyway, but we continue to figure out God's work and tell Him how to get it done. I hate to tell you this, but God doesn't need your coaching. He wants your prayers, but not your advice.

Because God worked one way in the past doesn't mean that's the pattern for the present. In other words: Don't put God in a box. When you put God in a box, it means you restrict His actions and destroy His options. You try to dictate how He should function. (I wonder if God laughs at the ideas of humans.) Isaiah says, "Ask Me of things to come concerning My sons; And concerning the work of My hands, you command Me" (Isaiah 45:11). That's not a verse to tell us to order God around. It's really a question more than a statement. This translation is closer to the intention in the Hebrew: "This is what the LORD says—the Holy One of Israel, and its Maker: Concerning things to come, do you question me about my children, or give me orders about the work of my hands?" (Isaiah 45:11, NIV). He goes on to say, "It is I who made the earth and created mankind upon it. My own hands stretched out the heavens . . ." (verse 12, NIV).

You don't have a choice about how, but you do have a choice to pray and to wait. And if you do, the fulfillment will surely come.

Don't give up hope. Don't quit praying and expecting. God is at work even if you don't see anything happen for a long, long time. (Remember Abraham.) Remind yourself of the five parts of Habakkuk's vision. The principles are the same for you and your vision.

1. It is for an appointed time.

2. It will speak.

3. It will not lie.

4. It will surely come.

5. It will not tarry (won't be delayed).

It doesn't matter where you are now. The promises are sure. God speaks; you listen. God cannot lie, for God not only speaks the truth, God *is* the truth. If you faithfully wait for the fulfillment of God's promises to you, it will happen. It will surely come. And when it's God's time for it to happen, nothing can delay it. That's the promise of God's faithfulness. If you do what you're supposed to do, God will do what He has promised. He gives the word of certainty.

God delivered the Israelites out of their slavery and God used

Moses. They left Egypt and expected to be in the Promised Land within a year. In fact, it took about a year for them to reach a place called Kadesh Barnea. They thought they were ready to move in and take possession of the land. But they weren't ready and God had to teach them before they were submissive enough to go forward. They grumbled and complained, but most of all, they didn't believe God. They had to wait another thirty-nine years before God acted. They had to wait until the faithless, nonbelieving generation died off.

God's promises are faithful, but they're not always immediate. That's the message you need to keep in mind. Just because it doesn't happen within two days doesn't mean it won't happen within a month.

Here's an example from the New Testament: Before he became a follower of Jesus, Paul (formerly called Saul) had received the authority to get rid of Christians in Damascus. He could imprison them or kill them, because the object was to get rid of all the followers of Jesus Christ.

On the way, God struck down Paul on the Damascus road. He was blinded and they carried him into the city. For three days he remained sightless, but in those dark moments, he became a follower of Jesus Christ. The Lord told Ananias to go and pray for him, but he also made promises about Paul: "Go, for he is a chosen vessel of Mine to bear My name before Gentiles, kings, and the children of Israel" (Acts 9:15). That is exactly what happened.

What we don't talk about was that the fulfillment didn't happen immediately. Paul went into the desert alone for three years. Even after he first joined the believers, many were afraid of him and he spent years proving his commitment to God. He made three missionary journeys and finally the time came for God's promises.

When it was the appointed time, Paul stood before King Agrippa. From the experience on the Damascus road until he stood before the king was about twenty years.

God did not lie. It happened, but it didn't happen immediately. It may be that way with you as well. But even if the fulfillment is delayed, it will happen.

It will happen!

60 SECONDS TO THINK

1. If you have stepped out of the boat, if you have waited and prayed, what is the vision God has given you?

2. Ponder the five things Habakkuk said:
- *It is for an appointed time.*
- *It will speak.*
- *It will not lie.*
- *It will surely come.*
- *It will not tarry (won't be delayed).*

3. What do you understand "appointed time" to mean to you?

4. Practice saying the following three words to yourself every day for at least a week—until you believe it: "It will happen!"

5. If you're willing to wait for the fulfillment of your vision, write your vision below. What do you want God to do for you?

5

Great Family Success

Several years ago I read an article about Alma Powell, the wife of former Secretary of State Colin Powell. As I remember the article, she visited a school in New York to speak to the students. She said the crowd of students didn't look friendly, but she went ahead and spoke anyway. She talked about her family and her children. Immediately, hands popped up everywhere.

She stopped and asked, "What's the question?"

"Mrs. Powell, what's a family?"

She was shocked and at a loss how to respond at first. She had assumed everybody knew the definition of a family.

Those kids didn't get it. They didn't get it because they had no families. Most of them were from single-parent homes (usually the mother) or were under the care of a grandparent or lived most of their young years in foster care.

"What's a family?" It's sad that anyone in the United States would have to ask such a question. The problem for those children was that they didn't understand the concept of family because they had never experienced the family—the kind of life we typically think of as being composed of the mother-father-and-two-kids.

When I think about that incident, I wonder if the family will survive into the future.

Today when you watch television, you see few family values projected and little evidence of the traditional family. If you examine the demographics within our churches, you may be surprised by the results. You might be shocked at the number of people who don't live by the biblical idea of family. I've been amazed at the number of children and young adults who have never seen their fathers or their mothers.

The concept of family isn't a modern arrangement, but is based on the principles established in the book of Genesis. All through the Old and New Testaments, the family is always the core. The family structure begins in Genesis 2. After God created Eve to be a companion for Adam, He says, "Therefore a man shall leave his father and mother and be joined to his wife, and they shall become one flesh" (Genesis 2:24). From there, God commanded them, "Be fruitful and multiply; fill the earth and subdue it; have dominion over the fish of the sea, over the birds of the air, and over every living thing that moves on the earth" (Genesis 1:28).

That husband-and-wife unity is no longer reflected in society. Even in our churches, about 50 percent of the members are single. Many of them are divorced; a few have never been married and don't think about getting married. The age of marriage is being pushed back and so is the birth of children. We used to assume that people married in their late teens or early twenties and had several children before they were thirty. Now people don't marry until they're thirty or thirty-five. Instead of the traditional marriage, the trend today has become the trial marriages where they live together for a year or more to decide if they want to marry. One man said, "That was my practice marriage." That has never been God's way.

When you study the media, what's coming on the airway is a total reprogramming of the family. Virtually every show has given you a view of domestic partnership, of being single. Shows today depict cohabitation without marriage and story lines of sexual promiscuity. Even music videos, many of which depict the exploitation of women along with inflammatory anger, are destroying the divine principle of the family. The lyrics of some of the music would make my parents blush.

But you don't have to let the media lead you and teach you values. You and I need to lead the media and turn them back toward a biblically based family. You and I can do that! You can make that 60-second choice and establish a great and successful family.

If you're going to make that decision to reclaim the family, the first thing you have to do is to pray for guidance from our Father so that you can guide your children.

Matthew records a story of a father who brought his son to Jesus because Jesus' disciples couldn't heal the boy. (Matthew 17:14–21. But see also Mark 9:14–29 and Luke 9:37–42.) The son was an epileptic. The father said, "He often falls into the fire and often into the water" (Matthew 17:15).

The boy was a victim of a satanic attack. In Mark 9:17, we read that the boy had a mute spirit. That spirit didn't come from God, so it must have been an attack from Satan. As I thought of that account, I realized that the attack wasn't on the father or the present generation. The attack was on the next generation. And that's why the disciples couldn't heal the boy. They knew only how to deal with Daddy's problems. They had already had experiences with the demons of Daddy's generation, but they weren't familiar with the attack on the next generation.

One of our serious problems today is that we adults, and many of us in leadership, aren't familiar with the attacks on the next generation and what's going on with our children. There is a war against your children and it has been escalating over the past decade. The worst part is that you probably didn't even know the war was taking place. You might be like me; I thought I was pretty up-to-date with the next generation only to be well-informed and embarrassed by my sixteen-year-old son.

One day I went to the weight room to work out with him. I have a CD player because music helps me to work out. However, I got tripped up that morning because I forgot to bring mine to the workout room. I'd done that before and once had to buy a CD player at the store next to the gym. About the third time I went to buy a CD player, I wondered why the selection of CD players was so limited and complained to a few of my friends about the store being so far behind that they did not even keep good CD players in there. "They ought to be more aware of what people buy," I mumbled to myself.

But on that particular morning when I planned to work out with my son, I had enough time to go home and get my CD player so I would have tunes while I worked out. When I got back to the gym, my son was already there on the treadmill. He had his headphones on, listening to his iPod. Hurrying to catch up, I took out a CD to pop into the player but in my rush I dropped it on the floor.

My son saw what happened and before I could grab the CD, he jumped off his treadmill. He picked up the CD, stared at it, and then at my CD player. "Oh, Dad, you're still into that?"

"Yeah," I said.

To his credit, my son didn't say anything more, but his tone of voice and the surprised look on his face answered a question for me. Now I knew why I couldn't find CD players in the stores. They've been around only a few years but they're already outdated. The kids are all into iPods and other technology that they can use to download, program, and even make music and movies.

As I watched him run on the treadmill listening to his iPod, I was shocked and amazed. Until then, I thought I was a pretty hip, cool guy hanging out with the young people and speaking their language and understanding their ways. But through that single incident, my son let me know I was so far behind that I didn't even know I had to catch up!

Later that day, I spotted someone taking pictures of his friends with a cell phone. That's common now, but it was a shock to me the first time.

I was out of touch.

But as troubling as my lack of knowledge of technological progress may be, what is truly frightening is that I had no idea about the messages and images these electronics may carry. I have since found that the next generation had been heavily attacked and I didn't even know an invasion had begun. Corrupt images and messages have attacked our children's minds and hearts and souls, and many of us parents aren't aware of this.

Since that workout with my son, I've asked questions, a lot of questions. I wanted to know the answers.

- How is the devil getting access to my kids?

- What is my son pumping into his head?

- What kind of things influence him and turn him away from Jesus Christ?

- Why do teens listen to their kind of music and not mine?

- Why don't they have the same values I have?

- How can I help them learn the true values of life?

That workout created a lot of issues with me. I don't go into my son's room, and I don't go through his things . . . yet, I know that many of the things on which he spends his time aren't spiritual. This troubles me but he's typical of his generation.

I tell you this story because you might think you're up-to-date but electronic technology is moving in such a fast way with its inventions and new forms of entertainment that the devil has great access to them but you, and other adults, don't even recognize it.

What can you do? How can you help to overthrow the attack on your kids? I can say this much: You and I aren't going to pull them back to our way of thinking or our kind of music or our values. But you and I can influence them and stand beside them as they make their way in the world. How can we help them, protect them, and overthrow the evil attacks? The first thing we have to do is acknowledge the battle and prepare our children so they will be mighty warriors in the fight.

Think about how you can prepare the next generation. I heard recently on a news report that state and county officials determine how many jails to build and how many cells within the jails *based on third-grade achievement test scores* because studies have found that a high percentage of those kids who can't read at grade level will one day sit inside those prison cells. That information shocked me because it means that the state has already determined the future of our children by the time they are in the *third* grade!

You and I don't have to let the state make those choices. We can help make changes, but first we need to make that powerful 60-second decision to say, "I will not surrender any more children to the prisons of America."

As I wrote this book, the media was filled with a story about removing more than four hundred children from a cultish, polygamous compound in Texas. Most of us were horrified at what went on, but I was struck by what one of the mothers from the compound said: "The world is so evil. We had to get away from the awful temptations around us all the time. People in your world are evil and we want to stay pure."

I don't agree with how those people were living, but I can understand that mother. For her (and perhaps for others in that group), she saw the encroaching evil and knew only one way to combat it: withdrawal from the world.

But withdrawal isn't an option. Yet, in a sense, that's what many parents have done: They've closed their eyes or ignored what goes on. I've unintentionally been one of those parents. Maybe you have as well. But once you have a sense of what is happening, you need to take action. You need to do something.

The problem is, too many of us ignore the problem. In the biblical account, the father said, "Lord, have mercy on my son, for he is an epileptic and suffers severely; for he often falls into the fire and often into the water" (Matthew 17:15). The father knew the boy suffered. He was determined not to allow his son to continue to be hurt.

Most church people haven't seemed to notice that their kids fall into "the water or the fire." Our kids are suffering, but we do nothing about it. Instead, we go to church, wear our best clothes, sing the gospel hymns, and pray for one another—and ignore our kids.

By the time the children grow up, some of them will have encounters with God. That's the good news. The bad news is that they have to spend the rest of their lives trying to get rid of the junk they picked up before they met Jesus. You are not guarding them in a relevant way to keep them from falling into the fire or throwing themselves into the water. By ignoring them or being unaware, they fall and you don't do anything to break the fall.

That epileptic boy had no control. Something inside him took over his body and his mind. This is much like kids today. They don't know why they do many things. They follow the crowd and do what everyone else does. They have no one to show them the right way. We must show them *that* way.

We're going to have to pray for God's guidance to show us how to do this. We need a new arsenal to fight this new evil. What worked for you and me twenty years ago and kept families safe from Satan's charms and powers just doesn't work today. We have to figure out what's going on around us and prepare for the onslaughts of the devil.

Before I was a preacher, I worked for the Ford Motor Company. Every year I was excited because we had a new car model and I would receive a new company car to drive. Every year they also shut down the factory for sixty days so they could retool. They did that because the old factory tools couldn't service the new cars. They had to stop production of the old and close up shop so they could get ready for the new.

We don't ever shut the churches down to retool or even pause to rethink whether we ought to keep doing things the way we did last year or twenty years ago. We just keep running them as we always have. We've got new people and we're trying to service them the way we were serviced thirty years ago. But those new people who are coming in, most with young families and teens, can't finish singing "Amazing Grace," because they never heard it. At most, they can mouth the first verse. They don't know the sacred hymns such as "Holy, Holy, Holy."

I'm not saying we don't need new music and new ways to worship. Maybe we need to keep up with the times. Why, we certainly worship differently than our parents did. I remember the time when no serious Christian man ever went into a church service without slicked hair, a tie, and a suit. I don't see much of that today—and I'm not protesting.

We can't push the young generation to embrace our music, and really, who's to say ours is better? An eighty-year-old friend helped me see that. He said that in 1943, he was listening to music of the big-band era, which was the music of his time. His father yelled at him and said, "Shut off those filthy songs." The man couldn't listen to popular radio at home so he heard the songs from jukeboxes and from the record players at the homes of friends.

When his own son was into rock-and-roll music in the 1970s he opened his mouth to yell, "Shut off those filthy songs," but he said he remembered the anger in his heart over his father not under-standing, so he said nothing.

"I tried to nudge my son in the way of values and talk to him. He turned out to be a pretty good Christian, but he's a baby boomer and looks at life through the eyes of his generation."

My friend went on to say that his son almost yelled at his teen-aged boy for listening to rap and what he called "gutter language." My friend said, "It happens with every generation. But I think this one has far more problems and temptations than I did, or even those of my son's generation."

We don't want to condemn the kids for wanting their own style of clothes, music, and entertainment. Their world is different and they don't even learn with the same methods we used. Instead, we need to integrate. We need to step into their world and be at their side during those times when they're attacked by the evil one. We need to be with them so that *we* can sing the new songs with them—the songs that are relevant for today, the kind that speak of values and principles.

If we will learn to sing their songs, they might learn to sing ours.

I once heard George Barna make a statement that went something like this: "Unless they learn early who they are by the grace of Jesus Christ, they will be lost in the sea of interchangeable identities."

Interchangeable identities. That's the phrase that grabbed me. It was also the first time I had heard the expression, but I understood what he meant. Before I was a committed believer, I was out there in the public places with all the others my age. I lived and worked in Washington, D.C., and I used to go to the clubs—just like most of the people I hung around with. After a while I got tired of the clubs. Someone called them the "meat market" and that's true. I got sick of going to clubs because I didn't know who I was meeting.

For example, I'd meet someone and we'd talk. It wasn't unusual for a man to tell me his name and that he worked for the federal government and was moving ahead on his career track. The next time I met him he'd have a different job and be excited about a new career. A young woman would be a college student who wanted to become a career diplomat. Another time the same student planned to be a flight attendant.

"Who are these people?" I asked myself. I realized they had no idea who they were. They changed jobs and were in and out of relationships. Nothing grounded them. They didn't know who they were. They didn't have any real identities. They seemed set and determined to follow a specific path one day but, a few days later, they heard another voice or saw another advertisement or a friend suggested a different road to follow. They'd think about the new way and get excited for a week or a month before they were ready to start something new.

When I was in seminary I read Martin Buber's *I and Thou*. He believed that God is most deeply known through relationship and said that before there can develop true relationship there had to be two separate beings who could relate. Makes sense to me. Unless we work to be ourselves (who we truly are), we can't know who we are, who others are, or the world in which we live, and most of all, we can't know God.

Our kids don't have to go through interchangeable identities. We can teach them who they are in Jesus Christ. As parents, we can't undo the lessons we have already taught our children but we can point them to God. Only after an encounter with Him will they be able to ask the right questions in life.

That is not what most of them do. Our children can grow up to be just like those people I met in Washington, D.C., and they will unless we help them change. The best help for change is firm, caring guidance by parents.

If you, as a parent, want your children to be different, you have to guide them. You are responsible. You need to be like the man who brought his afflicted son to Jesus. You have to set aside those 60 seconds to make the choice to heal the upcoming generation.

Too many parents excuse their absences and lack of teaching by saying, "I just don't have time."

That's not true. Every parent has the same number of minutes. You are just like the rest of us when it comes to time. It takes only one minute—just 60 seconds—for you to make that crucial decision. In 60 seconds each parent can determine to train and lead his or her own children. You can throw away the time, abuse it, ignore it, and it's only one, tiny, fleeting minute. It's 60 seconds, but eternity can be in those 60 seconds.

The church is at a crossroads of the very existence of the people of God, the very existence of a borrowed society. If we don't turn, we are only a generation away, forty years or less, to becoming a people who do not know the God of our fathers. Our children aren't turning to the God we love and serve. Something is wrong. They don't know how to face the struggles of life aided by Jesus Christ. They don't know what it costs to get them to where they want to go.

Because we don't pass on the faith and the faithful teaching, we are throwing away our families.

Some people say, "It doesn't matter." But it does matter. You can make that change for your family right now—*right now* within the next 60 seconds.

Of course your life is busy—too busy. It's always hustle, you're always working, always going after wealth or prestige or something else besides the basic thing you're supposed to do: Teach your children.

This isn't just something I've figured out on my own. It's not a new message that I decided to teach. This has always been the struggle with God's people. Thousands of years ago, the psalmist wrote this for his generation—and it's a message just as needed (and perhaps more so) by us today: "For He established a testimony in Jacob [Israel], And appointed a law in Israel, Which He commanded our fathers, That they should make them known to their children, that the generation to come might know them, the children who would be born, That they may arise and declare them to their children, That they may set their hope in God, And not forget the works of God, But keep His commandments" (Psalm 78:5–7).

Psalm 78 is worth emphasizing because it talks about four generations:

1. Generation one: their forefathers.

2. Generation two: their forefathers' children (themselves).

3. Generation three: the present generation's children.

4. Generation four: those children yet to be born.

And in keeping with this we understand that God always identifies himself as the God of Abraham, Isaac, and Jacob. Listing
those three names is a way to remind us that God is generational.

Think of the promises in the Bible that involve generations.
Although there are many, here are a few:

- To Abraham, God promises, "As for you, you shall keep My
  covenant, you and your descendants after you throughout
  their generations. This is My covenant which you shall keep,
  between Me and you and your descendants after you" (Genesis 17:9–10).

- To Moses and the Israelites when He explained the Passover,
  "So you shall observe the Feast of Unleavened Bread, for on
  this same day I will have brought your armies out of the land
  of Egypt. Therefore you shall observe this day throughout
  your generations as an everlasting ordinance" (Exodus 12:17).

- To the people of Israel just before they entered the Promised
  Land, "Therefore know that the LORD your God, He is God,
  the faithful God who keeps covenant and mercy for a thousand generations with those who love Him and keep His
  commandments" (Deuteronomy 7:9).

- To the people of God, "Walk about Zion, And go all around
  her. Count her towers; Mark well her bulwarks; Consider her
  palaces; That you may tell it to the generation following"
  (Psalm 48:12–13).

- A promise to all Israel, "Blessed is the man who fears the
  LORD, Who delights greatly in His commandments. His de-

scendants will be mighty on earth; The generation of the upright will be blessed" (Psalm 112:1–2).

If we miss this generational connection, we miss the biblical concept of family and the concept of generational families. God doesn't speak only to us and stop. We not only enjoy the blessings and peace of God, but have the responsibility to continue to pass it on to the generations that follow. That has always been God's plan.

Let's focus on the time of Nehemiah because I want you to understand what I call the "Nehemiah mind-set." First, a little of the history. Because of their sinful ways, the people of Israel had almost been wiped out. Most of those who survived had been carried into Babylon for seventy years. At last the King of Persia, who conquered the Babylonians, decided to let the Jews go back to rebuild Jerusalem. Ezra, the prophet and priest, led the first group. They built the city but they didn't get to finish the walls. Without walls, enemies of the Jews could attack at will. Nehemiah, who was the king's cupbearer, received permission and provisions from the king to build the walls.

Despite opposition from local people, Nehemiah went to build the walls. At the same time they were building, he and the others had to ward off any attacks by the enemy. Nehemiah wrote, "So we built the wall, and the entire wall was joined together up to half its height, for the people had a mind to work" (Nehemiah 4:6). They had a mind to work because their leader had the right attitude and they followed his example.

"The mind to work" means that Nehemiah and his people were

determined. They were there for a purpose and they refused to be frightened away and wouldn't give in to their enemies. He was there to lead the Jews to do what God had placed in his heart and mind to do.

Years ago I read a book on the rules of war. One thing stuck out in my mind. It says that a true victor does not go into a battle to see if he's going to win. He goes into the battle to live through the fulfillment of his vision, which is victory. A great leader sees the end before engaging in the battle. Good leaders know exactly what they want to see happen before they lead their troops one step toward the battle.

So remember that when you have a mind-set to win and to work, don't do it because you want to see if you can do it or find out if you can be successful. Dream the big dreams, see the powerful visions, know what you want to happen, expect the victory, and then go into battle. The victory needs to be in your heart before you take any distinct action. That's the mind-set of Nehemiah.

Nehemiah and his people faced constant opposition from Arabs and Ammonites, but they didn't stop or give in. At one point, Nehemiah listed the names of the enemies of God and wrote that when they "heard that the walls of Jerusalem were being restored and the gaps were beginning to be closed . . . they became very angry, and all of them conspired together to come and attack Jerusalem and create confusion" (Nehemiah 4:7–8).

He stated that they prayed and set people on watch day and night. And the people of God prevailed. Because of the Nehemiah mind-set, the walls were built and the people lived in safety. Never forget that victory begins in the mind.

What are you willing to do to make your family successful?

What are you willing to do to make your family honor God? The decision begins with you. Whatever mind-set you have will show up in those who follow.

I want to shift right here and point to one of the saddest statements in the Bible. It's the story of Jacob and his family. Jacob was favored by the mother, Rebekah, while Isaac, the father, was partial to Jacob's twin, Esau. That favoritism led to division and hatred within the family. One day, after Esau returned from hunting, he was hungry and wanted the stew Jacob had cooked. Taking advantage of his starving brother, Jacob demanded the birthright. As the firstborn of the twins, the special blessing of birthright belonged to Esau but he sold it for food. Later, Rebekah conspired with Jacob to deceive Isaac into blessing Jacob instead of Esau.

Jacob followed the pattern he had learned at home and deceived Laban, his father-in-law. He also favored his second wife, Rachel, over the first wife, Leah, and showed partiality to Rachel's son, Joseph. Jacob is a parent with twelve sons and probably just as many daughters. Again, following the mind-set of Rebekah, he favored one son. That was Joseph, his son by Rachel. Because of his preferential treatment, Joseph didn't have much of a chance. Jacob's mind-set had the boy already in place for his older brothers to despise him. According to the biblical accounts he was a tattletale and not a very likeable kid.

In a state of anger, the brothers sold him to a company of Ishmaelite traders who passed through the land. They took Joseph to Egypt and sold him there.

After they sold Joseph, the sons had to cover up their crime so they lied to their father. They said that a wild animal killed their brother. When he heard the news, it was a sad moment for Jacob.

Because he thought Joseph was dead, this is what the Bible says: "Then Jacob tore his clothes, put sackcloth on his waist, and mourned for his son many days. And all his sons and all his daughters arose to comfort him, but he refused to be comforted, and he said, 'For I shall go down into the grave to my son in mourning.' Thus his father wept for him" (Genesis 37:34–35).

Why is the statement sad? It's sad for two reasons. First, Jacob was a bad father. He never handled his children well and he spoiled Joseph. Because of the father's unfair treatment of the older brothers, those same brothers sold Joseph into slavery.

Second, Jacob remained a bad father. He was so consumed by his personal sense of loss and grief he wouldn't allow his other children to comfort him. For Jacob, Joseph was the one son that mattered. He didn't realize that he had eleven other boys and many girls. The brothers were alienated from their father because they couldn't grieve for the brother they despised; Jacob was alienated from his sons because he wouldn't allow them to comfort him. He shut them out of his life.

I can imagine that each of the other sons thought, *He wouldn't cry and groan like that for me. Only for Joseph.* That probably made them even gladder that they had gotten rid of their brother.

Sad, isn't it?

Jacob was the grandson of Abraham and the man who would become the father of Israel's twelve tribes. He blew it—not just once but every time he made decisions about his sons. He never took those 60 seconds to look at his own children or his own responsibility to them. He never considered them and their needs. Jacob was all about Jacob.

Too many parents are like Jacob. They openly prefer one child or another. Or as parents they detest their own sisters or brothers and their kids know it. As parents, if you respect some and disrespect others, you're a hypocrite for not loving all of them. But worse, the children watch you, see how you behave, and you become their role model for behavior. You teach your children the wrong values. By your lifestyle and attitude you say, "It's okay to hate some members of the family. They're not important anyway." You wouldn't say such words, but your actions made such an attitude permissible for them to copy you. And you come to church and wonder why your family is messed up. That's one reason: *By your actions*, you teach your children who to like and who not to like.

That's an important lesson you should have learned from the bad influence of Jacob. That man was a street hustler with big plans. He knew how to cheat and deceive, and was out to win regardless of the cost. He built up a fortune but he hated his twin brother and ignored his kids. That's the kind of father they grew up with. I wonder if that's not a good reason for God to get Joseph out of the clutches of his despicable father so he could change and become the man God intended him to be. Joseph had a lot of hard times in his life before he became the advisor to Pharaoh. If his father had been a better parent, life might not have been so hard for Joseph.

In Genesis 37, Jacob felt like an old man and he looked back on his life. His kids reminded him, "Papa, we're here." They don't say it, but I like to think they tried to tell their dad that they loved him and wanted to feel his love for them. But Jacob never changed.

Jacob doesn't hear them because he can't. He hadn't heard them in the past, so why would he hear them now? He didn't care about his other sons and daughters. He could only cry and mourn and weep over *his* loss. "How can I ever be happy again? How can

I rejoice?" If he were truly aware, he might have admitted, "I messed up in my own life and now I've screwed up another generation." But Jacob isn't that introspective or perceptive. He can think only of his great loss. His other children seem to mean nothing to him.

His other sons, like their father, don't operate with integrity either. The Bible shows us the action of two of them. There is the story of Shechem, a Hivite, who wanted to marry Jacob's daughter Dinah, whom he had already "defiled," as the Bible puts it. But he loved her and wanted to marry her. When Shechem and his father asked for Dinah in marriage, the Bible states that her brothers "spoke deceitfully" (Genesis 34:13) and tricked the Hivites into circumcising all their males.

"Now it came to pass on the third day, when [the Hivites] were in pain, that two of the sons of Jacob, Simeon and Levi, Dinah's brothers, each took his sword and came boldly upon the city and killed all the males" (Genesis 34:25). That's not all: "The sons of Jacob came upon the slain, and plundered the city . . . They took their sheep, their oxen, and their donkeys, what was in the city and what was in the field, and all their wealth. All their little ones and their wives they took captive; and they plundered even all that was in the house" (verses 27–29).

The end of that incident is that Jacob got angry, but not because they murdered the people or because they had done something wrong. Again, all the anger is really about how this affects him: "Then Jacob said to Simeon and Levi, 'You have troubled me by making me obnoxious among the inhabitants of the land . . . and since I am few in number, they will gather themselves together against me and kill me. I shall be destroyed, my household and

I" (verse 30). He never thought of their welfare or safety—only his own.

Yes, Jacob had taught his sons well. Part of that unconscious teaching was not to accept responsibility for their actions. The account ends with their response to Papa Jacob: "But they said, 'Should he treat our sister like a harlot?'" (verse 31). They don't seem to realize that they had murdered innocent people. It was all about *them*, but that's because they had learned that self-centered lesson from their dad.

There's another incident a little later where one of Jacob's sons, named Judah, promised to provide his youngest son as a husband to Tamar, who had been married to two of his sons. Both of them died but left no children. Under the custom of the land, called leverite marriage, when the first son died childless the next son had to marry the widow and raise children under the name of his dead brother. Judah promised that when Shelah, his third and youngest son, was old enough, he would marry Tamar. Judah conveniently "forgot" his promise. After waiting for years for Shelah to marry her, Tamar tricked Judah into having sex with her, conceived, and confronted him with what he had done. To his credit, Judah did say, "She has been more righteous than I, because I did not give her to Shelah, my son" (Genesis 38:26).

What do we learn from these stories? Jacob taught his kids— and they learned well. He obviously didn't intentionally teach them to deceive, lie, or cheat, but they learned by his example. They planned to kill Joseph but decided to sell him into slavery instead. Nice boys, right? There are probably hundreds of other things they did that dishonored God. But they learned to sin boldly from Daddy Jacob. Why not? That was the example for them to follow.

We're not much better today. Our children don't even know who to ask about living right. Instead, they listen to peers, to the voices on their cell phones and from the Internet. Our children struggle and we as parents need to pause for just 60 seconds and decide how we're going to make the changes that will turn their lives around.

They have questions and we're not giving them the right answers.

- What's wrong with copying another kid's paper? Everybody does it. Why not copy research from the Internet? Who will know?

- Should I finish high school?

- Should I go to college? Which college? What's wrong with lying on my application?

- How am I going to make a living?

- Who am I going to be when I'm grown?

- How am I going to make my money?

- Who am I going to marry? Or should I marry?

- Can I marry and still have a career?

- Can I be a career girl in a man's world?

Those are normal questions, but the young people ask the wrong people for the answers. Instead of going to their parents, they get the answers from their peers. They don't ask their parents because they can't get straight answers from them. They might get lectures; they might be ignored. They may hear, "I'm busy now." But they don't get answers, at least not godly answers. And many of them have parents who are Christians.

Our kids are troubled. They ask about whom to marry and they don't even know who they are themselves. Many of them are like Chevrolets who go to a Ford dealership. At the Ford dealership they don't have authorized parts or trained people to fix them or understand their identities.

Before they can ask questions about whom to marry, they need to discover their own identity. What do they want in life? What does God want to do in their lives? We've got jacked-up marriages because they don't know who they are and they're trying to find their identity in each other. They don't realize they can be complete in themselves. Too many of them seek partners to make them feel whole. One relationship doesn't work so they try another and then another.

They watch their parents and don't see wholeness there. They watch movies and videos and get caught up in a variety of things, but they still don't know who they are.

When they talk to their parents, too many of those mothers and fathers are like Jacob, but few of them will say, "I messed up my child. The mess-up has married another mess, which has piled it higher and deeper and it keeps getting worse and worse and they don't even know to call on Jesus."

A couple of years ago I saw a film starring Will Smith and his son called *The Pursuit of Happyness*. Smith wasn't just being an actor in a film. He also was raising his son to follow him. It took Will Smith more than twenty years to get started and achieve his goals. He has now advanced his son.

I'll say it more plainly. Your children shouldn't have to take thirty years to get where you are. If you have lived the right kind of life and followed your Strategic Life Plan,* their lives should have been speeded up because you took the time to teach them your values. You need to teach them values while you're living your life so you can advance them along the road and they won't have to take that many years before you pass them the baton. And then you can sit back and watch and see them grow.

When I think of generational issues, it often reminds me of cathedral thinking. I've seen a lot of cathedrals in my travels throughout Europe. Centuries ago, when a community of people decided to build cathedrals to honor the Lord, they built them so well that many of them still dot the landscape across Europe. I've seen a few such cathedrals that are close to a thousand years old. It also took the people about a hundred years to build a cathedral.

When people decided to build a cathedral, the process only started with that then-present generation. Their task was to plant trees. That may strike some as strange, but this shows the effect of generations. What's that got to do with a cathedral? Simple. That first generation started the foundation. They knew they wouldn't see it fully erected, but they got the process started for the next generation. They also gathered stones and other building material for those who followed.

The second generation came along, used the collected stones,

* See chapter 11.

cut down some of the trees, put up the walls, and finished the buildings.

The third generation took the rest of the trees that had been planted by the first generation, cut them down, and made the furniture that went into the cathedral. If nobody had thought of finishing something that was started by the first generation then it never would have gotten done.

I hope you'll think about that three-generation building project. You can be the children of your parents. You can be like those who taught you and follow their mistakes and their weaknesses.

Or you can decide to be the parents of the new generation. You can begin the family legacy that will continue on through your grandchildren and great-grandchildren. Your decision will take only 60 seconds.

I want to make it clear that not every parent has failed. There are many mothers and fathers who do a wonderful job of raising godly kids. I don't want to make the good feel guilty, but I would like to make the guilty feel conviction. I want to awaken all of us adults to care about the generation following us. I want us to pray and to fast. We can make a difference in their lives.

60 SECONDS TO THINK

1. For 60 seconds, reflect on your childhood and the training you received. What positive messages did you receive? What negative messages?

2. What positive messages have you passed on to your children?

3. What is one thing you did not receive from your parents that you wanted?

4. If you have children, what positive steps have you taken so they won't live with indistinguishable identities?

5. Make a 60-second decision to listen to your children—really listen. If you don't have children, why not spiritually adopt some and make that 60-second decision to listen to them? We all need someone to listen to us. Be that kind of person for someone else.

6

60 SECONDS FOR THE

Next Generation

I f you had 60 seconds to decide what to do for the next generation, what would you do? How could you use your time, your energies, and your gifts to reach to the generations that will follow you?

As you think about these questions, I want to point out the disconnect between generations. Here's an example. The generation of those who lived during the Second World War knew the atrocities committed by the Nazis in Germany. A sign at the gas chamber in Dachau (outside Munich, Germany) reads in four languages: NEVER AGAIN.

Yet a generation after the Second World War, the father of Anne Frank complained that the people had forgotten the atrocities of Hitler's regime. Anne Frank was a young Jewish girl who lived in the Netherlands and wrote a diary between 1942 and 1944 that became a classic for its time. But today, many people have no idea who she was.

We find the same situation all through history and all through the Bible. In the book of Judges, for instance, the Israelites failed God and their enemies conquered them. "When all that generation had been gathered to their fathers, another generation arose after them who did not know the LORD nor the work which He had done for Israel" (Judges 2:10). They cried out for help and God raised up men and women to deliver them. The taste of victory lasted about as long as that judge or deliverer lived. After a while, however, the people forgot the bondage they had known and drifted back into sin.

In the Bible, we also read of Joseph, the son of Jacob, who saved Egypt during a time of severe famine. Pharaoh gave the people of Israel some of the best land in the nation. A generation later, we read these words, "Now there arose a new king over Egypt, who did not know Joseph" (Exodus 1:8).

We find that sad commentary all through the ages. Time after time, another generation arose that didn't know the God of their fathers. Whether you call them generation X or Y or Z, you are now living in a different culture—and some feel as if they're in a new land. It's a new mind-set—a different way for people to operate and make decisions.

If you care about those who come behind you, one of the first decisions you need to make is to get in sync with the next generation. You don't have to look like them or act like them. They don't want that anyway. Don't imitate them. Instead, guide them. You need to understand their thinking. We're already losing them because too many adults refuse to open up to them. Too many adults judge, condemn, cajole, and belittle the present generation. (How quickly they have forgotten their own experiences of being judged by the generation before them.)

That's not what our young people need. They need your acceptance; they need your approval. They yearn for your love. They need your commitment to be so loving that you'll reach out to them, even if they don't know how to respond. To get in sync with them takes 60 committed seconds to decide. It takes 60 seconds to make that decision to reach them. And it probably won't be easy.

For those of you who aren't part of that generation, you need to remind yourselves that your world is dead. You now live in the world of iPod noise, YouTube, Facebook, text messaging, instant messaging on computers and cell phones. That's as much of their culture as camcorders and CB radios were of those of the previous generation.

Part of that decision to reach the next generation means you need to accept them just as they are and without their having to do something to win your approval. Don't condemn them because they behave or dress as they do. Don't yell at them because they use words that you would never have said at their age. They're only acting like everyone else around them.

Instead of condemning, you need to learn to incorporate them within your worship, your homes, your community, and your country. If you care about the next generation, you can't be judgmental baby boomers and expect them to accept your values.

Here's another thing you need to ponder: How can they accept your values when they don't understand the way you worship or how you communicate? They didn't grow up with typewriters or waiting days for a letter to reach a destination and another three days for the response. They know words like *instant, simultaneous, virtual,* and *multitasking.* They truly are the generation that doesn't remember Joseph or anyone else.

For example, the best-known Christian of the past fifty years has to be Billy Graham. Any baby boomer knows that name. Recently, I was with several people and one adult said, "I got saved under Billy Graham."

One teenager stared at him for several seconds before he asked, "Who's he?"

Someone else asked what group he played with.

That's an example of the generation gap, but it also means that if you're willing to make that commitment to reach them, *you have to change.* You have to open up. You can't expect them to know Billy Graham, and most adults probably don't know if Mercy Me is an expression or a singing group. But the young people of today know.

The conflict is that you don't realize how much tradition has made you comfortable in your walk with God. You have forgotten your struggles as a young person. You went through the awkwardness and pain of growing up and finding your own sense of identity. The next generation doesn't understand where you are or the problems of your generation. But then, you don't understand where they are.

If you make that one-minute decision to reach out to them, it means that you have to release a lot of the old things. You don't release your values or your standards, but you do have to let go of your way of doing things. Push away the negativity toward them.

Because you've done worship one way doesn't mean that's always the way it has to be. It doesn't mean it's the best way; it means only that it's the way you've done it most of your life.

As you reflect on your methods and your way of doing things, you need to ask yourself why you do things that way. How much of what you do came from the generation before you? How many of your standards are cultural and how many of them are truly Bible based? You need to look for a way to communicate with their culture so that you can become a welcome and active part of their lives.

Like a lot of adults, I'm constantly amazed not only at change but at the rapidity of change. Thirty years ago we didn't have cell phones. We not only had dial-up phones but they were rotaries. It cost us ten cents a minute to call across the country. We stood in line at the post office while now we can make our own stamps through the Internet. We used to buy heavy volumes of Encyclopedia Britannica, but today it's all online and we only have to make a few keystrokes. People are reading and downloading on Kindle and many adults have no idea what one is.

That means the world has turned to a totally different way of communicating. In our church service, for instance, we used to have someone stand up and read off a list of announcements. Now we do an e-blast. At one time we had telephone committees to get out the word about important events, but today we have electronic phone calling. We record the message and it's all done for us automatically.

I've made enough of an issue about your need to get with the present generation. Now I want to tell you about two pastors that have figured it out and are doing it—and doing it with excellence.

First is Craig Groeschel, the pastor of LifeChurch in Edmond,

Oklahoma, with satellite churches in Arizona, Florida, New York, Tennessee, and Texas, as well as half a dozen in the Edmond area. He preaches each Sunday at the main location and broadcasts to the other churches. That means every church has a local pastor and its own music and praise. Each has its own worship band. But he does the preaching on a giant screen. That's modern technology at work.

The amazing thing I learned from him is that except for one church, all the others have grown phenomenally over the past few years. The only one that didn't grow is the home church: the place where he preaches.

He has tapped into a different way to communicate and worship. I don't know all the facts, but it seems to me that the people are more interested in coming to see the preacher on the big screen than they are in sitting in the church building and watching him live.

Those churches also major in only a few things such as youth and children. Their focus is limited, but what they do is outstanding. They have learned to communicate with today's generation. For example, Craig Groeschel might say, "I'm going to speak to you about sex." Along with that he might do a little skit—a short, dramatic piece—or show a mini-movie. It's all done professionally. He's a good actor with a well-written script and the result is arresting. He and his staff act out the mini-movie, which he uses to launch into his message.

Groeschel spends the major portion of his time working on his weekly messages and filming them. He also notifies the camera crew and the pastors so they have an idea of what he plans to do and they can coordinate their energies. The creative material makes people laugh. Sometimes they cry. But they're always excited. Groeschel knows how to connect with the next generation.

The old method of the preacher who stands in front of a pulpit and preaches and teaches without input from the congregation isn't working for the next generation. They are used to something on the screen, whether it's a small screen or a large one. They're into the interactive kind of thing. Their attitude says, "Pull me in so I can relate."

Second is Rodney Combs. He's the pastor of a three-hundred-member church in Rockford, Illinois. Although he has been the pastor only about three years, Rodney has it figured out and has made the message interactive. He's not speaking to a swarm of people; he speaks and communicates with individuals.

Rodney prepares a message and stands up to speak. "We have designed our stage to look like a coffeehouse. On one corner of the platform sits someone on a sofa with a computer and cell phone.

"We assume that everyone in the congregation either has a cell phone or is near someone who does," Rodney said. "They can ask questions while I preach. We call this Why-Fi: Answers in Real-Time as a way to play off the technology and the idea that people's questions drive the messages."

He says they may not do this forever but it has become a core part of "how we do church. It gets better and better every week and the people love it.

"We do an interactive question and answer. I sit on one of the couches and often invite a few other people up to dialogue live with me while I continue to speak to the congregation. During the week we also use our blog to follow up and to keep the dialogue going before and after the message."

Here's a sample of the topics they've covered recently:

- What Makes Christianity Better Than Any Other Belief System?

- Where's the Good God in the Bad Stuff?

- What Do We Do When We Think the Bible Is Wrong?

- How Would Jesus Vote?

Although the two methods are different, both men show openness. How many pastors would announce, "Today I'll speak on sex"? Some would be embarrassed and some wouldn't know what to say about sex that would be meaningful and informative to this generation. How many would say, "Interrupt me with your questions"? But the next generation needs information and guidance. If they don't get it from the church, they'll get it elsewhere.

The next generation talks openly about the facts and fantasies in their lives. They're used to expressing their innermost thoughts on MySpace or YouTube. They don't seem to hold back anything, not even their attitudes and activities that involve sexual relationships.

The growing churches are typical of those where the leaders intentionally use the expression "stay on time." That has nothing to do with when they start the worship service but it means to stay on time with the people. Where are the people right now? How do I develop my thoughts for these people? What do they need that I can bring to them?

It's not that revolutionary. That was Jesus' whole thing. He shocked the people of his day, but He understood His listeners. Back then, He used the oral storytelling method. Storytellers of the ancient world were good and people gathered around them. Many good teachers spoke in parables, images, and fables that captured the attention of the people. Jesus used that method for one reason: It worked for His day and for the people of an agrarian culture.

Today Jesus would probably be on TV, star in a megaproduction on FOX, do an e-blast, or something revolutionary like that. I'm sure of one thing: He wouldn't be a typical televangelist. I firmly believe the TV evangelists served a purpose in one generation but they're not the people who touch the under-thirty crowd. Jesus would have a special way to grab people where they are and He would speak to the areas of their lives where they hurt.

Jesus was always relevant to people who were hurt and needy. Think of some of his encounters recorded in the Gospel of John. I've put these in my own words to express the message Jesus spoke to them:

- The woman at the well (John 4). "I know why you hide and why you're afraid."

- The blind man (John 9). "I know your isolation from others."

- The man at the pool (John 5). "You think you can't be healed, but I can heal you."

- The woman taken in adultery (John 8). "I know your sin-filled life and I forgive you."

- The stone throwers who wanted to kill the woman (John 8). "I know who you are. If you can boast that you haven't sinned, you get to take the first swing."

Jesus used the methods of his day and they worked. "[Jesus] entered the synagogue and taught. And they were astonished at His teaching, for He taught them as one having authority, and not as the scribes" (Mark 1:21–22). Because His message was right, He knew how to touch hearts, and the method was right, so that gave Him the authority He needed. He spoke with authority.

Today, technology is the vehicle. We have a wonderful opportunity to rule the airways. The churches that are starting to rule the airways are those that capture the people. They use the methods that work with today's generation and they're already figuring out how to reach the generation that follows them. Because they connect, people listen. More and more people tune out the old-fashioned styles. Notice I wrote *tune out*—that's how they say it today. We used to say, "They no longer listen."

I struggle with this issue every day and often pray about how to reach the next generation and the generation after that. I don't want to see this great church go on the decline after I retire or die. I expect it to grow and to keep on growing—and it will if I accomplish what I need to do to touch the next generation.

I have at least two mind-sets in my church—which is probably true in any church. We can't neglect the present and former generations. They need us. But we can't focus on them at the expense of the next generation. How can I respond to people who came to Jesus Christ before the days of television and who resent the Internet? How do I reach out to those who want the old hymns of the faith and hate the choruses and praise songs? They are the church. They were the foundation for many of today's congregations.

I don't want to neglect them but I also want to make sure there is a new generation to replace them. I can't yell, "Get off the stage. You had your time." They're as special and as loved as those belonging to the upcoming generations.

I know how to reach my generation. I learned many of the values and attitudes of my peers. It's easy enough for me to communicate the gospel to my peers.

"But how do you deal with the next generation?" someone might ask.

That's the second mind-set I encounter. They're the ones who want the new and the technological because that's prevalent in their daily lives and in their jobs.

I'm still learning, but I've come up with a few ideas. First, I have to stay in touch with the old but I have to be open to the new.

Second, through teaching and strategic planning, I can process things to reach the newer people on this earth. For example, I invited Craig Groeschel to preach to my congregation. He began to integrate his perspective and principles into my congregation. I have since used some of his mini-skits in my messages and to test the market with my folks to see how they accept that. I've had mixed reactions.

Should I have expected differently? No, both mind-sets are at work and I'm sympathetic to both. And I care about both groups.

When I know I'll have to be away on a Wednesday evening, I've tried Rodney Combs's method. Instead of inviting a preacher to come, I've recorded a message and had it projected on the big screen. To my surprise, it has gone over well. People respond just as if I'm there.

Consequently, I've started a slow, strategic indoctrination to incorporate and use other methods and innovations. I don't know how much I can personally integrate, but I'm going to try because a long time ago I made that 60-second decision to reach out to the next generation.

Here is something else about how this works: In 2002, we started a church in Charlotte, North Carolina—about three hundred miles away from our home base in metro Atlanta. After that we started another church in Savannah, Georgia, which is about half that distance from the east side of Atlanta. The two churches already have a combined membership of ten thousand, so we believe we're doing something to connect with the next generation. We've also established a church in Concord, California, and another in Spartanburg, South Carolina, and will soon have one in Greensboro, South Carolina. I mention these because our next step is for me to do satellite hookups with Charlotte. If this is as successful as we expect it will be, we'll have the mother church telecast to other churches. I will start feeding myself into my various churches.

Our vision is beyond the borders of the United States. Our vision incorporates the world. We also plan to reach out to the next generation by starting five churches in Africa, three in the United Kingdom, and we've targeted two for France. We have to work out the differences with time zones and coordinate the technology, but this is our vision and we believe we can make it happen and still be relevant to the people of this and the next generation.

Third, I'm trying to listen. I want to hear the articulate of the younger generation and I want to hear those who can't put their needs into words, but they sense when they're accepted, when they're merely tolerated, and when they're completely, though politely, rejected.

6O SECONDS TO THINK

1. This chapter begins with the question: If you had 6o seconds to decide what to do for the next generation, what would you do? Take those 6o seconds right now and ask yourself not only what you could do, but what you are willing to do.

2. In this chapter, I talked about outstanding people in one generation being forgotten by the next. Will you do something practical to keep your memory alive? You might write about your values and how you learned them. You might want to record what you've learned. How about a video where you answer this question: What do I want you to know and to remember about me?

3. If you could speak one sentence to the younger generation that you would want them to listen to and live by, what would you say?

4. Take 6o seconds and ask yourself: "Am I refusing to get off the stage and let the next generation take over? Do I criticize them because their generation is not like mine?" Take another 6o seconds and ask yourself: "What did I reject from my parents' generation? How are my values or even style of worship different from theirs?"

5. The young need your approval and love. What is *one action* you can take that says, "I accept you and love you"? What did you wish your parents had said to you when you wanted things to be different?

7

60 SECONDS TO

Commit to a Plan

We can learn so much if we look at that small Old Testament book called Habakkuk. The prophet started out with some big questions. He couldn't understand how God would let the sinful nation of Israel be overwhelmed by the Babylonians who were even more sinful. He had questions and he cried out to God for answers. Habakkuk was frustrated and confused because the wicked prospered and continued to prosper and grew stronger every day while the people of God were constantly cast aside. Israel was wicked but the Chaldeans (or Babylonians) were more evil, yet they defeated God's people. Nothing good was going on for Habakkuk and for God's people.

I knowingly take a little liberty with this material because I want to make it personal for you as a reader. Let's see if this works for today. Suppose a man comes to me and says, "I don't know why stuff isn't working for me, Bishop. I come to church, I go to Sunday school, I attend Bible study, I pay my tithe, I put my few dollars in the love offering, and stuff just ain't working for me."

Here's how I'd answer: "Yes, but you haven't *done* anything. You have come to the buffet. You *eat* the word, but you don't *work* the word."

It was the same during Habakkuk's time. Half-committed saints and wicked folk were doing better than the faithful of God. So the people of God ask, "How long, Lord, will you let this go on?"

God doesn't answer, so they decide, "Okay, I'll get involved. I'll go to all the special services at church, give a big offering. I'll even pray. Maybe then God will do something for me."

Does this sound familiar? It does to me. I hear that a lot, especially at the end of each calendar year. We have New Year's Eve services, and for many, New Year's is kind of the shout of "all clear" after a fire drill. It's a resuscitator. After twelve months, people are worn out and need somebody to give them new hope.

The people who cry out don't have a plan. Or they have some vague idea of how they want to live. They're too busy crying out, "Why am I suffering?" They also ask, "How long am I going to suffer?"

I can answer both questions simply and easily:

1. You suffer because you don't have a plan.

2. You'll suffer as long as you don't have a plan.

Let's look at God's answer. Habakkuk 1:5 reads, "Look among the nations and watch—Be utterly astounded." He goes on to say that He is going to raise up the Chaldeans [Babylonians] who He calls "a bitter and nasty nation." God says they will prosper. They will triumph. Imagine that! God's people had failed. They did a lot of bad things and God says, "Okay, I'm going to raise up really bad people and they'll conquer you."

That doesn't make sense to you, does it?

It didn't make sense to them either, but it does to me. They failed because they were the chosen people and yet they planned their lives without God. They turned to their own ways and ignored their Creator. These aren't the words the prophet wrote but this is the meaning: "You won't ignore Me any longer," the LORD says. "I'll make life so miserable and hard for you that you'll cry out, beg, and plead for Me to help you. When you're that desperate you'll hear from Me."

Is that much different from where you are today? Some of you are miserable. You're in debt. You hate your job. Your wife (or husband) wants to leave you. Your kids despise you. You see no way out of your locked-in life. It looks as if every evil force has come against you.

Guess what? You're exactly right. Everything *is* working against you. And those forces will continue to come against you until you do it the right way—until you do it God's way.

I wish you'd see this as a moment to lay down your book, get quiet, pray, and focus on hearing God. Listen and hear what He has to say. But don't listen unless you're ready to hear and then to act on what you hear.

Let's look more closely at Habakkuk. His vision took place in the realm of the Spirit. Futility and frustration comes when people attempt to solve spiritual problems with natural answers or with only their brains without engaging their hearts. You need to see things from God's point of view—from the perspective of heaven and not from the earth's point of view.

You've got to get up and look down instead of being down and trying to look up. There was no vision for the people until the prophet moved to a higher level and transcended his present circumstances.

Turning totally and completely to God is the only way to make life changes. You cannot solve your problems on the same level as your problems. You have to get above them. You have to move up to a higher point of view and a higher authority.

In Habakkuk 2:1, the prophet cries out, "I will stand my watch And set myself on the rampart, And watch to see what He will say to me." As I read that verse I was reminded of people who get others to pray for them. "Oh, pray for me because . . ." One reason they ask is that they're too lazy to pray for themselves.

Although it's good to have others pray for you, the real deal is this: You have to do some things for yourself. That's exactly what Habakkuk tried to point out. "You want other people to do things for you that you should have done for yourself," he tries to tell them. "It won't work." The prophet said he was going to stand on the rampart and wait for God to speak to *him*. He didn't wait for someone else to explain God or God's will. He determined to get it directly from God Himself.

I'm a pastor—a bishop—the leader of a wonderful, large congregation. I want to help people. That's one reason I'm a preacher and pastor. But I can't do everything for everybody. Even if I could, it would be the wrong thing for me to do. Each of us needs to do for ourselves whatever we can do for ourselves. Beyond that—and only after we've done all we can do—if we need help, we can ask.

That's a strong principle of the Bible and that's one reason you and I need to have a word with the next generation. If they see that you stand on the rampart and that you watch and wait for God to speak, you can influence them as well. You set the example.

I feel so strongly about this that about two years ago I made a decision: I won't help people in my congregation who refuse to have a plan. I grew weary of Christians who came to church and groaned about how badly life treated them.

"Do you have a plan for your life?" I asked one man.

"Uh, well, no. I'm in such bad shape I can't—"

"No, you start with a plan," I told him many times. "Once you start with a plan and work your plan, your life will change. Don't try to change things without first having a plan."

To others I've also said, "If you don't have a plan, you're not ready for my help. You're not ready for anyone's help. If you don't have a plan, it means you don't want to help yourself. You may say you do, but if you have a plan, you can get somewhere. Get the plan going and then I'll help. Others around you can help. But you have to start with your plan."

I made that decision and it's like the old story about giving people fish and they can live for a day or you can teach them to fish and they can live a lifetime. So here's the message I began to live by and to preach: We aren't giving away any more fish. We are willing to teach you to fish so you can continue to eat, but we're not going to catch the fish for you.

I mentioned a plan—and in the chapters that follow, I'll explain more about the plan. But it begins with that 60-second decision. It begins with two words. Those two words are "I will."

I'd like you to pause right now and go to the exercise at the end of this chapter. Under number 1, write these words: "I will plan." You may need to write those words several times or at least read them aloud until they become a part of you. That's your first 60-second decision: I will plan.

For the second line, I want you to write, "I will . . ." and finish the sentence by writing just one thing that you're going to do as part of that plan. It may be as simple as setting aside time to pray and think about the plan. It may mean dropping out of activities that use up your time and your energy. It might mean turning off the TV an hour earlier in the evening.

If you can determine to do one thing for yourself, you're ready to move on to the next step. If you're going to run ahead and get out of your mess, you must have a plan and you must determine to follow it. Do it the way Habakkuk did it. Another translation reads, "I will climb up to my watchtower and stand at my guardposts. There I will wait to see what the LORD says and how he will answer my complaint" (2:1, NLT). That's the number 3 of your plan: "I am going to isolate myself and get away from everyone else until I work out my plan. I am going to go wherever I need to go or do whatever I need to do so I can hear from God."

Write on the third line what you will do to climb up into your watchtower. It doesn't mean you have to go somewhere for a week. It means that you will go there long enough and often enough that you can hear God speak and tell you what you need to know and to do.

Or maybe you already know. Is that possible? Sometimes you may ask God and beg for guidance but you already know the answer. You keep crying because you think that maybe if you cry long enough and loud enough, you'll get a different response or maybe

God will change His mind. God isn't going to change; you have to change.

Make that 60-second decision to stay in the watchtower. Don't stop. Keep listening. The closer you get, the more your mind will tell you to give up. Instead of quitting, say to yourself, "I can't stop. I'm real close right now. I can't stop. I can't faint." I remind myself of Paul's words, "And let us not grow weary while doing good, for in due season we shall reap if we do not lose heart" (Galatians 6:9).

If you truly start with "I will plan" and keep on going, God will be with you. You may feel as if you're trying to walk on water, but don't be afraid. Jesus grabbed Peter after he took his first steps on water and started to sink. Jesus' hand is strong enough to grab yours as well. You won't sink. You won't fail because Jesus won't let go.

60 SECONDS TO THINK

1. Write your determination and your commitment. Write these three words: "I will plan." Write each letter carefully and say the three words aloud as many times as you need.

2. Finish this sentence: I will establish a plan and I will . . .

3. As you complete this simple exercise, ask yourself: "How difficult was it for me? Am I afraid I can't stay with a plan? Does this sound too easy and I'm bound to fail?"

4. What is one thing God wants you to do? Can you answer that question now? If not, continue to pray until you know. God will show you.

In the pages that follow, I'll help you strengthen yourself so you can establish a plan and stay with it. If you're willing to make the commitment, that's all it takes right now.

8

60 SECONDS TO

Advance the Kingdom

Jesus didn't come to preach Jesus. He came to proclaim the kingdom of God. He announced that the kingdom of God had arrived.

Before Jesus' arrival on the scene, John the Baptist hollered and told listeners to change their minds and their way of living. "The kingdom is here." He wanted them to know that. Those words meant that the ruler of the kingdom—Jesus—is here. "Repent, for the kingdom of heaven is at hand!" (Matthew 3:2). John meant that the kingdom was almost there because Jesus was almost ready to start His public ministry and bring God's kingdom to earth.

During the early days of His ministry, Jesus sent out His twelve disciples and instructed them, "As you go, preach, saying, 'The kingdom of heaven is at hand.' Heal the sick, cleanse the lepers, raise the dead, cast out demons. Freely you have received, freely give" (Matthew 10:7–8). Like John the Baptist, those twelve announced

His imminent arrival. It's likely the disciples didn't know exactly what they preached, but Jesus did.

When Jesus came, He did what no one had done before: He took authority over all the powers of evil and darkness; He healed; He set people free. That power arrived with Him and He passed many of those gifts on to His close followers.

That hasn't changed. The kingdom came with Jesus on earth. The kingdom remained on earth after He went back to heaven. Through our church, we have a TV program called *Taking Authority*. We called it by that name because we have been charged to subdue nations. That is, to go after nations and spread the gospel of the good news of the kingdom that Jesus and His followers established on earth.

Jesus brought in a new order but too many have gone back to the old ways. There are always those who want to build private kingdoms and grasp power to control others, but that's not the kind of power Jesus meant. His kingdom is a realm of service. His kingdom is about being like Jesus, who got on His knees and washed His disciples' dirty feet (John 13).

A new order is here. And there has to be one church—many congregations but one people—and we have to start working together instead of building personal kingdoms on different corners and fighting with one another or boasting about who has the largest following. The kingdom isn't about saving souls (although that's both basic and important) and it's certainly not about grabbing members from other churches. The kingdom of God on earth is about God's people coming together to change the world and doing what we do best in our own corner of the world, and we do it regardless of how many members are in our fellowship.

If someone can do something better than we can, we need to submit to that person or that ministry. We need to do whatever we can to get things done for God. What we don't need is to say, "If I can't have it, I'll see that he doesn't have it either." Those are not the words of the kingdom.

The challenge here is to preach, teach, and live so that others know we're part of the kingdom. Our lives as well as our words can get into the minds and hearts of people. It's not a mind-set of entitlement we need but a mind-set that says the earth and the fullness thereof belong to the Lord. As a leader, I have a mandate to become everything that God ordained me to become.

My role is more visible than most people's, but my role isn't unique. I may stand publicly before thousands, but I also stand privately alongside everyone else. Isn't that the same mandate for every believer in every church in every country in every time period? If you live like people of the kingdom, you change. You don't stay the same way you were. You push away the pettiness, the selfishness, the me-first attitude.

Think of it this way: If you change, you can change your family. You can change your community. You can change your city, your state, and even your country. Think how that would work if every one of us followed that mandate!

This chapter asks you to take 60 seconds to advance the kingdom of God. What can you do in 60 seconds? *You can decide.* You make a decision that affects all eternity. That's the point of each of these chapters. If you decide to advance the kingdom, the first thing you have to do is quite simple: *You must take rulership over yourself.* You have to put your own life in order. You can't advance the kingdom until you have advanced your spiritual life.

That's not a call to attend church more or do more of anything. It is a call to be more given to Christ, more open to the Holy Spirit to speak to you. It means living a holy life and, as I've pointed out earlier, others will know you by the way you live.

Jesus warned, "Beware of false prophets [or false Christians], who come to you in sheep's clothing, but inwardly they are ravenous wolves. You will know them by their fruits" (Matthew 7:15–16).

You don't have to be in the church long before someone says, "You're the only Bible some people will ever read." You know the problem with that statement? The problem is that it's true. If you live in ways to contradict the gospel of the kingdom, you can be sure there are people who will know. Many of them haven't entered into the kingdom themselves but they surely know what kingdom members look like and how they behave.

I wonder how many Christians have done wrong and been rebuked by nonbelievers for their wrong actions. Those same people often end by saying, "And you're a Christian, too."

Maybe you are a Christian, but you don't act like one.

That should not be the case.

Make that decision to live so that you honor God every minute. Decide to do what you can to advance the kingdom of God.

Do you want to advance the kingdom?

The obvious answer is yes, but I want to ask it again: Do you truly and honestly want to advance the kingdom? If you say yes, it won't be easy. Take the next 60 seconds and ponder this question before you answer: What must I do to get ready to advance the kingdom?

If you decide to advance the kingdom, it doesn't matter if you're a deacon, an usher, whether you sing in the choir, or direct traffic in the parking lot, that's good. It's just not enough.

I don't mean that you have to do more *inside* the church. I mean you have to do more *outside* the church. God wants you active and visible in the marketplace, in your job, on the bus, driving in traffic, or at sports events. Wherever you find yourself outside the church doors, you are operating as a representative of God's great kingdom on earth. Everything you do and everything you say needs to reflect the grace and love of God that brings others to the kingdom.

Does that sound like hard work? It is. You'll have problems—that's just part of being alive in the world. You won't ever be free of problems. But you can choose the kind of problems you have. You may be disliked, hated, or persecuted for being righteous before God. And if that happens, Jesus has a word for you: "Blessed are those who are persecuted for righteousness' sake, For theirs is the kingdom of heaven. Blessed are you when they revile and persecute you, and say all kinds of evil against you falsely for my sake. Rejoice and be exceedingly glad, for great is your reward in heaven, for so they persecuted the prophets who were before you" (Matthew 5:10–12).

Even when you try to do the right thing, everyone won't applaud you. If you have understood God's love and grace in your life, however, you will respond differently than other people. You'll have as many heartaches, setbacks, and struggles as anyone else (maybe more). But you'll also have the peace that comes from knowing you're doing the right thing.

"And have you forgotten the encouraging words God spoke to you as his children? He said, 'My child, don't make light of the Lord's discipline, and don't give up when he corrects you. For the LORD disciplines those he loves, and he punishes each one he accepts as his child'" (Hebrews 12:5–6, NLT).

Because you claim the name of Jesus Christ, you also take on yourself the responsibility to represent Him and to honor Him. When I was a boy, I often heard parents exhort their children, "Remember your name. You do right and honor your name when you go out in public." They were saying, "If you do anything wrong, it involves more than you. You not only shame yourself, but you bring shame on the whole family."

The principle is the same. Your shame as a Christian reflects on every child of God.

I want you to understand something about advancing the kingdom that unbelievers don't understand. If you have hard times, it's not because God is against you. You don't have to cry out, "Why, God?" You already know why. You know you need to learn lessons. You know you need to be cleansed or spiritually renewed. You know you need to grow up spiritually. The roadblocks and difficulties are loving actions from God to help you move forward and advance the kingdom.

You also know that even in your darkest times, not only is God with you, but that's when you become the most effective witness of God's grace in your life.

Whether or not you're aware, you influence people all the time—for good or bad. Nothing seems to advance others' concept of the kingdom more than when they see that you have your personal world under control, when they see you can take hardship and still declare, "God loves me."

And here's something else about advancing the kingdom: None of God's kids can say, "I'm nothing. I'm nobody." You can point to your lack of education, your gender, your race, your poor job—you can always find reasons to prove you're nothing. The one thing you can't disprove is that God says you are somebody. God says He loves you and created you. That's what makes you worthwhile. You are somebody right now.

If you belong to God you're important and God's mandate to you is to get control of your life so that you can focus on helping others enrich theirs. You can't help them if you don't have yourself in order.

Does that sound like hard work? It is. You'll have problems—that's just part of being of this world. But once others know you are a kingdom man or a kingdom woman and live as a member of that kingdom, those who are outside the walls of God's kingdom will see a difference in the way you respond to what goes on around you. If you respond like a kingdom person, you advance the kingdom. You show who you are and to whom you belong. You can make a difference in people's lives—and often in ways that you won't ever realize.

Cecil Murphey tells of the time he and his wife picked up three children every week for Sunday school and church. Their parents weren't interested in going but the children said they wanted to go to Sunday school. It was twenty minutes of extra driving, but he and his wife went. One Sunday, fourteen-year-old Tina, the oldest of the three, came to the door and said, "We ain't going today."

He asked them to call him when they wouldn't be able to attend. They promised they would. A few Sundays later, they didn't call and they didn't answer the door when the Murpheys arrived.

Over the next six months, the kids never called and about half the time they didn't come to the door.

About a year later, the Murpheys left that area to go to Africa as missionaries. More than six years later, they visited their hometown. They visited old friends and were preparing to go out to dinner. A young woman came to babysit for their friends.

She smiled at the Murpheys and said, "You don't remember me, do you?"

They admitted they didn't.

"I'm Tina," she said. When they still didn't make the connection, she reminded them that for nearly two years they drove to her house every Sunday. "After you moved away, we missed you. No one else wanted to pick us up because we lived too far away. We never forgot what you did for us."

Tina went on to say that three years earlier she had faced a big problem in her life. "I remembered the way you two talked about God all the time. He was so real to you. I started to go to church because I wanted to find that real God for myself. I wanted to find the God that you two had." She beamed as she said, "All three of us kids are believers. And the main reason is because you went out of your way Sunday after Sunday, even when we hid behind the drapes and wouldn't let you take us."

That's advancing the kingdom and we do it in all kinds of ways, but mostly we do it by living the life of the kingdom—by being who we are and operating with integrity and honesty. And we can't live the kingdom life until we get our own lives in order.

* * *

Here's another thing I want to point out about advancing the kingdom: Once you pause for 60 seconds and make that decision, God holds you to that promise. That's not a threatening God, but a loving Father who wants only the best for you. Sometimes you have to get spanked or beaten up to get straight, but God does it out of love.

Think about the story of Moses. From everything we read, we can assume he knew God wanted him to lead the people out of their slavery and into the Promised Land. His mistake was that he rushed ahead, got angry, and killed an Egyptian. That wasn't God's way.

When Moses learned that people knew what he had done, he ran away in fear. He spent forty years of running and hiding among sheep. One day the Lord said, "Okay, you have a mandate on your life. This is the time to fulfill it."

Like a lot of us, Moses objected. "Who am I? I'm nobody. I can't do this. I'm just one person. I can't talk, I don't have anything. Why are you bugging me?" He had all the excuses ready, but God didn't listen to his whining.

You can read the story in Exodus 3, and it's a lengthy dialogue in which Moses argues with God. I laugh sometimes when I read that: Didn't he know no one can win an argument with God?

Then I stop laughing because a few times in my life I've behaved the same way. I didn't feel worthy or good enough or smart enough. I felt like nobody. Maybe it's all right to feel that way until God grabs you and says, "From now on, you belong to Me, and I have a job for you. That makes you somebody."

It's also as if God says, "Enough. I have a job for you. I need you to leave the sheep right now, leave Midian, and leave all your painful memories of failure. Go back to Egypt and get My children and set them free."

Moses came up with one more excuse: "What if they don't believe me?" (See Exodus 4:1.)

Instead of answering the question, God showed him the answer. "What is that in your hand?" (verse 2). It was a shepherd's rod and God told him to throw it on the ground, and when he did, the rod became a snake. That got Moses' attention. God told the man to reach down and grab the snake's tail. When Moses did that, the snake became a rod again. God is the God of miracles (when needed) and he wanted Moses. He was willing to do whatever it took to get Moses on the job.

It's interesting that Moses never said, "But, uh, you know, uh, I killed a man back there and Pharaoh probably wants to kill me."

Even if he had used that excuse, it would have been worthless. Maybe Moses was smart enough not to say that. I know, however, that a lot of people look back at their past as a reason to say, "I'm worthless. I'm not worth forgiving."

Excuses didn't work for Moses. Why would they work for me? Or for you? Or for anyone? One of the things each of us needs to do is to get comfortable with our history. You can't change your past. Isn't it amazing how much time some people spend in regretting and visiting the past? You might be one of them. You go over the words you said or the things you did. You think if you go over them enough times they will go away. But they don't go away. In fact, the more you rehearse them inside your head, the stronger they become.

Even though they don't go away, God forgives you. God wipes away your past. That's who you were then; this is who you are now.

If you face your history, no one can use it against you. Your mess is your own mess. But that mess is what becomes your message. Your history gives you strength. You know how bad you were and you know what God has done. He cleaned up the mess and turned the message into a sacred message.

Moses must have been able to go from mess to message or he never would have gone to see Pharaoh. The man who had been a shepherd for forty years because of a mess he made was able to stand up to the king of the land and say, "I'm here with a word from God."

No matter how insignificant you think you are, when you look back over your history you'll see that's also where you'll find strength. The strength that took you out of your mess is the same divine strength that equips you with a message.

If you know the story of Moses and Pharaoh, you know the king wasn't impressed at first. Moses came and tried to stand up to him, but the king made life even harder for the Hebrews. Finally, God sent Moses and Aaron back to face the king. Aaron threw down his rod and it turned into a snake. Pharaoh's sorcerers and magicians threw down their rods and they also became snakes. But God had the last word: "For every man threw down his rod, and they became serpents. But Aaron's rod swallowed up their rods" (Exodus 7:12).

Each time Moses returned to the king, he was stronger. He was there to advance the kingdom and he had pushed his mess behind him to deliver the Divine message.

That's how it works—from strength to strength. Think about King David as an example. He was the youngest of eight sons and a shepherd. One day he killed a lion that attacked his sheep. Another day he killed a bear. That was his preparation for the bigger things ahead.

Later David visited his soldier-brothers and heard Goliath challenge them to come after him. David was apparently only a kid—a teenager probably. King Saul doubted his ability and said, "You are a youth, and [Goliath] a man of war from his youth" (1 Samuel 17:33b). David stood up firmly for himself. He was a young man, but one who knew his message. He also knew the source of his strength. Before he went against the giant of a man, he asked, "But who is this uncircumcised Philistine, that he should defy the armies of the living God?" (1 Samuel 17:26).

When he stood up to fight Goliath, the young warrior didn't back down. "Then David said to the Philistine, 'You come to me with a sword, with a spear, and with a javelin. But I come to you in the name of the LORD of hosts, the God of the armies of Israel, whom you have defied. This day the LORD will deliver you into my hand, and I will strike you and take your head from you . . . Then all this assembly shall know that the LORD does not save with sword and spear, for the battle is the LORD's, and He will give you into our hands" (verses 45–47).

David knew his God and he knew the power of God. You know the end of that story and the youth's victory over the enemy. The victory is also yours. When you build on your past and you live with strength in the present, you may not literally kill giants, but you become a blessing for the future of others. You advance the kingdom, even if you never say anything. You advance the kingdom because you live like a citizen of the heavenly kingdom.

60 SECONDS TO THINK

1. Do I want to advance the kingdom and am I willing to do whatever it takes to advance the kingdom?

2. What is at least one thing I must do to get ready to advance the kingdom?

3. Pause for 60 seconds and think of the things of your past that trouble you. As you name them, say these words, "Today I am free from my past. Today I am free from my past." You may need to say the words several times, but they're true, even if you find them difficult to believe.

4. What is one thing I can change in my life? What is one small, simple thing that will become the first step toward advancing God's kingdom?

9

60 SECONDS TO

Empower and Change

In seventh grade, I took an achievement test. Weeks afterward the school counselor called me to his office. Without trying to water it down or say it kindly, he looked directly at me and said, "Eddie Long, you're too dumb to go to college."

I don't think I had said anything about going to college. How many kids in seventh grade think that far ahead? He told me, "Perhaps you might look at other educational resources." That was his way of saying to me, "You're too dumb to do much in life, so just get along the best you can. Play sports until you finish high school."

You know what? I believed him. I stayed in school when I might have dropped out after a year or two. My parents wouldn't have let me quit, so I played sports. I was pretty good at them—not great or outstanding, but good. So I stayed on to graduate from high school because I played football and ran track. Our principal loved the athletes and he let us get away with just about anything. I could cut class or even take my friends to the office and he'd say, "Hey, Eddie, how about the game Friday?"

"Got it," I said. "We're going to win!"

School was fun, but I didn't take it too seriously. I was too dumb to think about college or anything beyond graduating from high school and finding a job. That's probably the way my life would have gone except for one person.

The high school guidance counselor, Miss Chapman, had always been nice to me but she was nice to everyone, so I didn't think she noticed me. About a week before I graduated, she asked me what I was going to do.

"Get a job. Make some money."

"No, Eddie, you're going to college."

"No, ma'am, I'm too dumb." My mind played back the words I had heard five years earlier.

"You are not stupid!" she said. "And you *are* going to college."

The way she put it, I didn't have a choice, but I wasn't ready to let go of that voice inside my head. She filled out the papers for me to go to North Carolina Central University and told me to be ready to start in the fall semester.

"If I'm going to college," I said and tried to joke with her, "God is going to have to take me there."

Miss Chapman didn't argue with me; she didn't even listen to me. "You *are* going to college."

In her mind, it was settled and I would go to college.

A few weeks later, I drove to the campus of North Carolina Central University because I had to take an entrance examination. I didn't know most of the information the test asked for. I sat in the chair and tried to read. I didn't even understand the questions, so I certainly had no idea of the answers. The entire examination was filled with multiple choice questions and I was supposed to color in the correct answers. We had one hour for the test.

I prayed silently. *God, if You want me to get in, You have to give me some right answers.* I knew I had little chance of passing the entrance exam without God's help. I prayed that a lot of those circles I colored were in the right places.

When the hour was over, I left and went home. I didn't expect to be accepted. Two weeks later, I received a letter from North Carolina Central University. They welcomed me as a freshman. I couldn't believe what happened. If I had doubted miracles before, I didn't doubt them then. God had to have helped me fill in enough right circles to get admitted to college.

I went to the university and began to apply myself. Four years later I graduated from North Carolina Central University. I tell this incident in my life because I was absolutely one of the last persons I thought should be in college. But because I believed God wanted me there and performed a miracle to get me into the school, I determined to study hard. To my surprise, I excelled in my classes.

I excelled because one person, a teacher named Miss Chapman, had believed in me and pushed me to believe in myself. She didn't take hours to lecture me. In less than 60 seconds she made me, a twelfth-grade student, aware of my destiny. She empowered me to step forward. She probably had no idea what she was doing, but her words and her faith in me empowered me to move forward.

I'm grateful to North Carolina Central University for accepting me, but I'm even more grateful to that guidance counselor, Miss Chapman. Her words changed my whole life. I am now the highest-giving personal donor to North Carolina Central University. I'm proud of that honor because they accepted me as a student and educated me when I didn't know how to believe in myself. Today I'm on the board of trustees of the school that accepted me. That means I can help dictate policy. That means I can help other kids who want to go to college but someone took away their power by calling them stupid, dumb, or made them feel they couldn't do it. Not everyone has a Miss Chapman in their lives, so this is my way to help.

Somebody spent less than 60 seconds—that short space of time—to empower me and to change my life. In those brief seconds, she empowered Eddie Long and changed the direction of his life.

Miss Chapman is not totally unique. You have the same capacity to empower others, and words spoken in just one minute can change lives. The more people you empower, the more valuable your minutes become. Say this sentence to yourself: "God wants me to be blessed so I can bless others." That self-empowerment can begin in 60 seconds. It begins when you say, "I will empower others."

I invite you—I urge you—to pause for 60 seconds. Examine yourself and ask a few probing questions:

- Who am I?

- Who has empowered me?

- Who spoke words of encouragement in those times when I felt discouraged?

- Who are the people who changed the direction of my life? What did they do?

- Of those who have encouraged or empowered me, who do I most want to be like?

- What does God want me to do to empower others? How can I increase the value of others?

Almost everybody knows the exploits and achievements of David, the greatest king of Israel. What many don't know or forget is his beginning. He was a shepherd and the eighth son of a man named Jesse. Apparently his brothers were good-looking dudes.

God sent the prophet-priest named Samuel to anoint a new king to succeed the unfaithful King Saul. "Fill your horn with oil, and go; I am sending you to Jesse the Bethlehemite. For I have provided Myself a king among his sons" (1 Samuel 16:1b). Samuel went and he met Eliab, the oldest son, and said, "Surely the Lord's anointed is before Him!" (verse 6).

Samuel was wrong.

"But the Lord said to Samuel, 'Do not look at his appearance or at his physical stature, because I have refused him. For the Lord does not see as man sees; for man looks at the outward appearance, but the Lord looks at the heart'" (verse 7).

Samuel passed him by and considered Abinadab, the next son, and when he did so, he realized God hadn't chosen him either. Samuel met seven sons and finally asked Jesse, "Are all the young men here?" (verse 11).

Jesse, perhaps apologetically, said there was one more, the youngest, and he was working among the sheep. The implication is that he didn't consider David to be outstanding.

Samuel refused to sit down for a meal with the family until they brought in the youngest son. When David appeared, Samuel knew. In that insightful, anointed moment, the Lord whispered to Samuel, and he anointed David to become the next king of Israel.

Let's think about that situation. Jesse had seven handsome sons—and apparently they were impressive. The story suggests that each one of them would have been an excellent, natural choice. By focusing on their good looks, Samuel almost made a mistake. It is fortunate for history that Samuel listened to God. God had chosen David, and Samuel anointed him.

It's hard to imagine how David felt. He must have wondered why he had been chosen when there were seven others ahead of him. Can't you see the eighth son, probably only in his teens, stare in shock and ask, "Why me?"

We receive no answer for that question except that God had chosen him. One thing that moment did for David—it changed his life.

The priest sent from God anointed David and the young man was never the same again. "Then Samuel took the horn of oil and anointed him in the midst of his brothers; and the Spirit of the LORD came upon David from that day forward" (verse 13).

That's what happens when you're empowered: You change. You see life differently. And you can never be the same person. Instead of "I'm too dumb" or "I can't do that," you shout, "I can! I can!" When one person—a teacher—believed in me, my life changed. I was empowered.

I want to tell you about a man I know who came from a poor family. He achieved academic success and did extremely well in the business world. One day he said to me, "I thought I was dumb. My five older siblings struggled through school and all of them dropped out before graduating. When I was in eighth grade, we had to start choosing classes for our first year of high school."

He said that he didn't plan to choose the track called college prep. When his best friend, Allen, saw his selections, he yelled at him. "You're smart! You're one of the smartest kids in our class."

"I am?" (He was, and almost everyone seemed to know that but him.)

Because of Allen, my friend changed from easy, nondemanding classes and signed up for the college prep courses. He didn't end up with the highest grades in high school, but he reached the top of his class in college and was second in his master's degree program.

"I don't know what happened to Allen," he said one day. "I heard that he dropped out of school in the tenth grade, but he changed the direction of my life." He added, "I think of him sometimes and my heart is sad. If only I or someone else could have empowered him the way he did me."

Again there it is: one voice. One person to empower—and it only takes one person who will devote 60 seconds to someone else.

No one empowered Allen.

One teacher empowered me.

What decision will you make within the next 60 seconds about empowering others?

60 SECONDS TO THINK

1. Who empowered you even in a small way? Write the name of one person who believed in you or encouraged you. Take 60 seconds to thank God for every person who has encouraged and empowered you in some way.

2. Who tried to take away your power by calling you stupid or weak or lazy? Pause for 60 seconds and ask God to forgive that ignorance and the pain those remarks caused you.

3. Focus on *your* opportunity to empower. Write the name of one person you want to empower. By encouraging just one person and genuinely helping that individual to be what God created him or her to be, you empower that one. It may be the first one, but let it be only the first.

4. Reflect again for 60 seconds. What is one thing you can do to empower someone today?

10

Prepare for Prosperity

People come to church and listen to what's preached. If they're ministered to, they're blessed. They're encouraged. And they grow. I want people to grow. However, sometimes people in the media attack me and call me a prosperity preacher. I don't cater to the media; I try to reach people where they are and where they hurt.

Yes, I am a man who preaches prosperity, but it's not prosperity as some people seem to understand. I believe God wants us to prosper *in everything we do*. Money is only part of that, but it is part. I want every aspect of your life to be enriched.

So I warn people: Don't allow people in the secular media to rob you of spiritual things. Don't let them cloud the issue by speaking against prospering. Their attitudes seem to want to justify poverty.

And some Christians believe that because they're poor they're blessed for having nothing in this world. They feel they have a special corner of God's grace because they're destitute, can't pay their bills, and have to beg God (and people) for food and clothes. I can't understand that. It's as if they think they're special for being unmotivated and unwilling to improve their situation.

People sometimes quote Jesus as saying, "Blessed are the poor in spirit" (Matthew 5:3), but Jesus didn't pronounce a blessing just because people are poor and want to stay that way.

I want to clarify Jesus' words in Luke 6:20, where Jesus says, "Blessed are you poor, For yours is the kingdom of God." In this case, He's speaking to those downtrodden and disenfranchised people of His day. They had few if any opportunities for advancement because of the vast chasm between rich and poor. The kingdom of God is not theirs because they are poor. It is theirs despite their poverty.

Some see the poor as the new chosen people. They suffer now and they can expect glorious blessings in the world to come. It's as if anyone below the poverty line gets to the doorway of heaven first. I don't agree.

That can hardly be the intention of Jesus' words. Jesus meant, "Even though you're poor, you're not invisible to God. He is aware of you and your needs." Jesus offers hope and joy to those who are impoverished. That's not the same as pronouncing a blessing on those who can't get enough to eat or don't have money to pay their bills.

So I want to be clear what I mean by a gospel of prosperity. And it is something for which I stand tall and without apology. I preach a message of financial and material prosperity because I live in the United States. I couldn't preach that aspect of the gospel in some impoverished, Third World countries, but there's no excuse for defaulting on paying our debts. Not in America. Yes, we have economic downturns, but I'm convinced that those who want to prosper can do so. You may have to start at an entry-level position but there is no reason you can't work your way up.

In another chapter I wrote about the Nehemiah mind-set. That's the determination to get a job done and to do it well and not be knocked down along the way. Nehemiah defied the enemies of God when he traveled from Persia to Jerusalem and rebuilt the walls of the city. His enemies plotted against him, but that man of God prevailed.

Prosperity works the same way. You can become prosperous in the United States if you determine to prosper. Of course there are forces that work against you. If it were an easy road to travel, everyone would be wealthy.

But you can prosper. If you have the Nehemiah mind-set, you can make it happen. And this isn't just a message for Christians. I've watched immigrants in this country for the past thirty years. No matter what country they came from, whether Laos, Russia, Nicaragua, or Zambia, if they came with the Nehemiah mind to work, they have prospered.

So why is it so bad or misleading if I preach about prosperity? I don't want to see people hungry and living in poverty. I want them to demonstrate to the world that the gospel works. If you work as the New Testament commands you, you will win.

Here's a command from Paul, written to those who were slaves—to men and women who didn't have the vast opportunities that we have in the United States: "Slaves, obey your earthly masters in everything you do. Try to please them all the time, not just when they are watching you. Serve them sincerely because of your reverent fear of the Lord. Work willingly at whatever you do, as though you were working for the Lord rather than for people" (Colossians 3:22–23, NLT).

That's the kind of prosperity gospel I preach. The message rings just as true today no matter who you are. If you substitute *workers* or *employees* for the word *slaves*, it seems clear what God expects of you.

I can't give you a better biblical example to follow than Joseph. He was sold into slavery. He could have spent his years yelling about the unfairness of life. He could have screamed that he was the son of a wealthy man in Israel. He could have refused to work or to do anything degrading. Don't forget, Joseph was the son to whom Jacob gave a special coat that set him apart from his brothers. He had been used to the higher positions in life. He might have had a number of slaves that worked for him.

Here's how the Bible describes the situation: "The LORD was with Joseph, and he was a successful man; and he was in the house of his master the Egyptian. And his master saw that the LORD was with him and that the LORD made all he did to prosper in his hand. So Joseph found favor in his sight, and served him" (Genesis 39:2–4a).

That's not the end of the story. But let's make sure you get this right. God was with Joseph. My question is: How did his master know the Lord was with Joseph? Doesn't it seem obvious? He worked hard. He did the best he could. He served his master with a total commitment. And he was a new slave!

The biblical account goes on to say, "Then [the master] made him overseer of his house, and all that he had he put under [Joseph's] authority. So it was, from the time that he made him overseer of the house and all that he had, that the LORD blessed the Egyptian's house for Joseph's sake; and the blessing of the LORD was on all that he had in the house and in the field. Thus he left all that he had in Joseph's hand, and he did not know what he had except for the bread which he ate" (Genesis 39:4b–6a).

Joseph is my kind of man. He exhibited the Nehemiah mind-set. Think about those statements. Look at the many times it tells us that the Lord was with Joseph. Or maybe we might say, "Because Joseph served the Lord with his whole heart, God blessed him in everything he did." The slave owner had to have seen something special in his new slave to promote him to such a position. Can we doubt that Joseph worked hard? That he was a man of honor? That he showed integrity in all he did?

You can be a Joseph today. If you give yourself to your work, regardless of whether it's sweeping the floors or hauling trash, God will be with you. You can prosper.

You only need to look around. God prospers those who serve.

Some people think it's sinful and shameful to be rich or even moderately well-off. They are wrong. Paul wrote to Timothy about that topic: ". . . those who desire to be rich fall into temptation and a snare, and into many foolish and harmful lusts which drown men in destruction and perdition. For the love of money is a root of all kinds of evil, for which some have strayed from the faith in their greediness, and pierced themselves through with many sorrows" (1 Timothy 6:9–10).

Paul didn't say money was the root of all evil, but *the love of money* is the problem. It's greed, it's putting the desire for wealth above all things.

So I want to make this clear: According to the Bible, there is nothing wrong with prosperity and financial success. It is the *love of money* or yearning for possessions that God despises. Paul says that such things become a snare. That is, a trap. These people have their minds and hearts set on the wrong thing. They trip and fall because they see only things and can't see God. That's the kind of wealth the Bible speaks against.

Prosperity in America, however, is available if you are prepared to succeed. God wants you to prosper in every area of your life. As you use your talents, God multiplies them, you prosper, and you bless others. The prosperity isn't just for you, but it's for you to share and to lift those who need a hand reached down to them.

Successful people maximize their minutes and allow no justification for poverty.

Perhaps this becomes clearer if I mention a story Jesus told about a successful farmer. "'The ground of a certain rich man yielded plentifully. And he thought within himself, saying, "What shall I do, since I have no room to store my crops?" So he said, "I will do this: I will pull down my barns and build greater, and there I will store all my crops and my goods. And I will say to my soul, 'Soul, you have many goods laid up for many years; take your ease; eat, drink, and be merry.'" But God said to him, "Fool! This night your soul will be required of you; then whose will those things be which you have provided?"'" (Luke 12:16–20).

That's the story but the real punch line is the question Jesus asked. He told the story because two brothers fought over an inheritance and he said, "Take heed and beware of covetousness, for one's life does not consist in the abundance of the things he possesses" (Luke 12:15). After he concluded the story, he let the two brothers have it straight in the face: "So is he who lays up treasure for himself, and is not rich toward God" (verse 21).

Those are the key words: *lays up treasure for himself.* That's the wrong approach. Nowhere in the parable does Jesus condemn wealth or say that it's a sin to be rich. He condemns wealth when it becomes a god for us, when money and possessions and the burning desire to possess more things take over our hearts. We do everything to get more and before long, our wealth and possessions control us. Jesus called that *covetousness* and that's what it is because it means never being satisfied with what God provides. Such people constantly grasp for more and more and more. No matter how much they get, they're never satisfied.

As Jesus said, "So is he who lays up treasure for himself, and is not rich toward God." You may gain money and possessions, but that's not the same as godly prosperity. Possessions aren't the final measuring stick of life. What counts most is a heart for God that's willing to work hard and faithfully to please God (and your employers).

By contrast, if you fully give yourself to money, to getting and accumulating and having more, the love of money drives you. That's not God at work in your heart. But if you understand that God wants you to be blessed, it's not just for you or me to boast of what we own. God blesses you and me so that we can use what we have to bless others.

At New Birth Church, we haven't spent all our resources on ourselves. We enjoy the prosperity and the blessings so that we can reach out and help others. Corporately and personally we've provided funds to build two hospitals in Africa. If we hadn't received God's financial blessings, we couldn't have been the source of blessings overseas and to the needy in the United States.

In Kenya, we took over a maternity hospital. Before we took it over and rebuilt it, they reported 80 percent of their newborns did not survive. Now we have the Bishop Eddie Long Maternity Hospital in Nairobi, Kenya, and the survival rate *exceeds 80 percent*. We did that within a space of two years because some faithful people in America decided to get rich enough so they could help needy people in Africa.

If you are an American and reading this, I remind you that God put you in the United States and wants to bless you and make you prosper. You're not in Zimbabwe where there's 90 percent unemployment. You're not in Darfur, which is overwhelmed by fear over ethnic cleansings. You don't live where you have to see raw sewage running down the street and there are no jobs available.

You are in America and if God put you in America don't let anybody tell you that you're supposed to be jacked up and it's not spiritual to prosper. God placed you in this country and at this time *because He trusts you.* He trusts that if He blesses you, you won't spend it all on yourself—you'll pass on part of that blessing to others.

This is one more time when you need to take 60 seconds. This time you need to choose to accept prosperity—but you do it so that you can become a conduit, so that the Lord will use you as a channel to pass on the blessings to others. Whatever God gives you becomes more than you need and you then become the source of blessing to someone else.

In one of his parables, Jesus told about servants who receive talents from God. (A talent referred to a metal weight. A talent of gold would be worth about two thousand dollars today, which was a fortune in that time.) All three men received different amounts, but that wasn't the issue. The issue was their faithfulness to use what they had. To the two men who acted wisely and invested his money, "His master replied, 'Well done, good and faithful servant; you were faithful over a few things, I will make you ruler over many things'" (Matthew 25:21).

Jesus provides financial resources to you today. You may be the one who makes minimum wage or you may be the highest-paid person per hour. It doesn't matter to God how much you earn; it matters to God how you use what you earn. It matters to God when you don't invest and earn what you're capable of.

When you're faithful with whatever God gives you—small amounts, large amounts—it doesn't matter. It's not the amount of the gift, but the way you use it that counts. You can multiply those abilities to bless folk who are less fortunate than you and to bring them into a place of promise.

Not only do I want you to take 60 seconds to make a decision, I want to point out that you have a responsibility to exploit where you are and what you have. It doesn't make you unspiritual when you have your mind set on kingdom things. If you go after the kingdom and His righteousness, God will add everything you lack and will give you all the help you need to accomplish your goals.

I like to point people to the wise words of Jesus in the Sermon on the Mount. Although the entire passage is worth quoting (see Matthew 6:27–34), Jesus made a powerful point of how to handle things in this life. He urged us not to fret over the things we need because He will take care of us. "Therefore I say to you, do not worry about your life, what you will eat or what you will drink; nor about your body, what you will put on. Is not life more than food and the body more than clothing?" (Matthew 6:25). Jesus pointed to nature and said God takes care of everything there, and we're of much more value. He concludes with another admonition that we're not to worry (verse 32): ". . . For your Heavenly Father knows that you need all these things." The verses lead up to one powerful statement: "But seek first the kingdom of God and His righteousness, and all these things shall be added to you" (verses 32b–33).

These are divine promises—right from the mouth of God to your eyes and ears. If God is truly first in your life, you'll have everything you need for the tasks you've committed yourself to do. And it's not just enough for yourself: You'll also have enough to share with others. You can because God provides.

Take those 60 seconds right now and make that decision.

Seeking the kingdom isn't dressing up for church, greasing yourself down every Sunday, or shouting praises. The kingdom means you study to show yourself approved to God. (See 2 Timothy 2:15.) One translation says it this way: "Work hard so you can present yourself to God and receive his approval. Be a good worker, one who does not need to be ashamed and who correctly explains the word of truth" (NLT). You study so you can understand God's word, but you also study to broaden your horizons, to educate yourself, and to develop your gifts so you can go after whatever God has put in your heart. But you've got to *know* what He put in your heart before you go after it. That is, you need to get focused on God.

Another thing you need to consider: No one—absolutely no one else in the world—can do what you can do. God has something that only you can do for Him. Nobody can mess you up if you know for what reason you're called and you know who called you. If you understand that, you can get up every morning and shout, "This is the day the LORD has made; we will rejoice and be glad in it" (Psalm 118:24).

You can shout, "Nobody is going to mess up my day because they don't control the day! God made the day and He made me for the day and He has a plan for me in this day to bless me and I shall follow that plan!"

"But, Bishop," someone cries, "you don't understand. Prosperity isn't for me. I make minimum wage and I've been making minimum wage for a couple of years."

True, that's not a lot of money, but it is money. It's money you earned by honest work. That's enough seed to start your move to prosperity. Your job on minimum wage may be like the servant with only one bar of gold. Others had more than he did and others have more than you do. But if you will work with your talent, *God will multiply it*. And I'm not talking just putting it in the offering. I mean using your gifts, as small as they may be, for God's kingdom, which is also for the good of others. Read and obey this word from Paul: "Work with enthusiasm, as though you were working for the Lord rather than for people. Remember that the Lord will reward each one of us for the good we do, whether we are slaves or free" (Ephesians 6:7–8, NLT).

Did you get that? You work for the Lord and not for the paycheck. You work with enthusiasm. You put your heart completely into your work. That alone will move you out of the minimum-wage line.

God has a plan for you. And His plan is more than helping you pay your bills each month. You have limits in this life but you haven't reached those limits. How can you know your limitation for income and influence until you stretch out beyond where you are now?

I became aware of great possibilities and pondered limitations one day when I walked around the site of the church property of New Birth Church. We've been greatly blessed and have a 250-acre complex. Because I'm not a surveyor, I don't know the exact boundaries of the property, but I know it's a lot of land. Somebody has marked it off and set the limits. You have to walk quite a distance to find the limits of New Birth property. As I walked around that day, I became aware that the property was a lot like you and me. You have limits—somewhere—but you don't know where they are in your life. I don't know my own limits. None of us do. We have to keep pushing and reminding ourselves that only God has staked the boundaries.

You have a territory that's larger than you think. But you've never sat down to check it out and to push the boundaries. And maybe there really are no limits if you serve a limitless God. If you push forward, you may find out that you don't ever have to stop until Jesus calls you into heaven.

I'm out of the first Adam and into the last Adam. That means I have tapped into the inexhaustible resources of God, which are in Jesus Christ, the last Adam. If I can think like God I can capture everything God has for me. But I've got to get myself quiet enough, settled enough, and determined enough to do what He ordained.

Pause right now. For the next 60 seconds concentrate on your limits. How many of those are truly your limits? If they're your limits are they also God's? How many times have you said you didn't have enough education, enough ability, or you weren't smart enough to accomplish something?

Some years ago a friend was afraid to try a computer but his boss forced him to take on the task. "If you work here, you'll have to use the computer." Once my friend understood what he was doing and lost his fear of the computer, he became a techie. Now he advises his friends when they face problems.

You can do it. You can do whatever you want if you allow God to direct you. Like Peter, you can look at the waves and despair, or you can move out and keep walking on the water alongside Jesus.

You can change your mind and your attitude. You know that and you've probably done it a hundred times. If you change your mind, you can also change your behavior. If you believe God will prosper you so you can prosper the kingdom, it can happen.

And it can begin today.

60 SECONDS TO THINK

1. For 60 seconds repeat these words: "I will become prosperous so I can enrich others in need."

2. Each of us is talented. To deny that talent is to deny God at work in us. Ask yourself, "What is one talent or ability God has given me?" (If you're still not sure, ask a trusted friend.)

3. Once you acknowledge at least one talent, ask yourself, "What is one thing I can use that talent for to help others prosper?"

4. Repeat these words: "God made the day and He made me for the day and He has a plan for me in this day to bless me. I will follow that plan!"

5. Please take 60 seconds to commit yourself to using your talents for prosperity. This isn't a commitment to be rich so you can accumulate. This is a commitment to prosper so you can enable others to prosper.

11

60 SECONDS FOR A

Strategic Life Plan

We started something at New Birth called the Strategic Life Plan. This is a plan that you can download from our website.

If you wish to download, follow these steps:

1. Go to www.newbirth.org.

2. Click on "News & Events" at the top of the page.

3. Select "Resource Center."

4. From there go to "Resource Listing."

5. Select "Strategic Life Plan."

This plan has already changed many lives, and it can change yours. First, I would like to tell you how the Strategic Life Plan came into being. It began because one member had a vision of what could happen.

HOW THIS BOOK CAME ABOUT

My name is Elder Angela Hill of New Birth Missionary Baptist Church. In 2006, Bishop Eddie Long preached a series of messages called "A Minute for the Next Generation." Through that series of messages the Lord used his words to admonish us to redeem the time, and to plan strategically for our lives so we could make a difference. He challenged us to leave a legacy—a generational legacy.

The messages stirred me so much that I felt we needed to take action and to do something about them. The result is the Strategic Life Plan (SLP) that we implemented at our church. The purpose was to teach us to leverage our resources—our life, gifts, talents, abilities, skills, and money. We also wanted to do it in such a way that we reflected the image of Christ in the world. We wanted each member of New Birth Church to leave a generational legacy—a legacy that lasts through more than one generation and continues to impact our world and our culture long after we're gone.

"Everyone ends up somewhere," Bishop Long has said many times. "Few people end up somewhere on purpose." He identified five areas and we have focused on them: Spiritual, Family, Financial, Health and Wellness, and Community and Civic Engagement. Throughout his pastorate, he has been consistent in emphasizing them.

1. *The Spiritual area challenges us to quiet ourselves before the Lord to identify the personal destiny and purpose He has already ordained for our lives.*

2. *The Family area encourages us to critically examine patterns of behavior and paradigms of thinking that have significantly impacted our bloodline and that will require us to commit to making decisions that will shape better futures for succeeding generations.*

3. *The Financial area urges us to examine our effectiveness as stewards, as well as to identify the talents, skills, and abilities God has given us to create and sustain wealth generationally.*

4. *The Health and Wellness area pushes us to become better caregivers of our bodies and to remind ourselves that our bodies belong to God. He also prompts us to seek wholeness in our emotions and mind.*

5. *The Community and Civic Engagement area urges us to examine the influence we have as Christ's witness in our local community, the state, the nation, and the world.*

Throughout the SLP, Bishop Long frequently refers to children and children's children. While some of those who agreed to follow the SLP aren't birth parents, all Christians are responsible to create a better future for succeeding generations. We also suggested that if they had no birth children, they might focus on the positive impact of SLP on nieces, nephews, cousins, godchildren, and any other children within their sphere of influence. We have also urged those who are married or are parents to create both a family and an individual SLP.

Another important element is that we set up SLP to include children and young people. We realized that their understanding would be different so we adapted the program to suit their age groups. Their involvement largely depended on their parents initiating the SLP. As parents work on their SLP with their children and grandchildren in mind, children automatically become a part of the SLP process. We soon learned (as we had hoped) that as parents led by example, young people thought about future generations and desired to complete their own plan.

At New Birth, we also arranged a special program called Super Strategic Saturday to assist people to complete their plans. We showed them how to set up and use the Strategic Life Plan Starter Kit.

For those who decide to try to do the SLP, I want to be the first to point out that it's not an easy, quick, one-day or one-year idea. It will take a lifetime to complete because it's a living document. While we have to invest a lot of time to create the plan, we also need to add to and modify it as our journey continues.

I can't stress enough the importance of the Strategic Life Plan. And as I continue to point out, it begins when you make that 60-second decision.

Within you and within your reach, God has equipped you with everything you need to be successful in life. As you consider this plan, I want to stress a few things that will help you.

- Make a commitment to write and work your plan.

- Set apart time daily or at least weekly to work on your SLP.

- Keep a notepad/journal close by to record the things God speaks to you.

- Enlist an accountability partner to keep you on track. (See chapter 12.)

I believe in the SLP for many reasons, but the best is the most obvious: It works. It's not a miracle plan and it's not an easy plan either. Before you jump into this, be sure it's what you want to do and are capable of continuing.

Over the years, it seems as if many of you stay on the slippery slope. You reach for things and just before you attain what you want, you slide downward. You stop yourself and start back up the slope. You take four or five steps forward, reach out, and then you slip again.

When you slip you can easily get lost—you fall into moral confusion, question your own integrity, and easily become cynical. Worse, you never seem to find a sure footing. You don't give up the desire to reach for the right goals, but you try to find them through the slippery slope. There are better ways to reach your goals and you don't waste a lot of energy and years searching.

That reminds me of Genesis 12. The chapter begins with the promise of God: "Get out of your country, from your family And from your father's house, To a land that I will show you. I will make you a great nation; I will bless you And make your name great; and you shall be a blessing" (Genesis 12:1–2). Abraham lived in Haran because his father, Terah, moved there with his family. But it's interesting that just before the promise, we read about that trip and

Haran was not the place they were to stop and stay: "And Terah took his son Abram [later Abraham] and his grandson Lot, the son of Haran, and his daughter-in-law Sarai [later Sarah], his son Abram's wife, and they went out with them from Ur of the Chaldeans to go to the land of Canaan; and they came to Haran and dwelt there" (Genesis 11:31). Terah died in Haran—he died before he reached the land promised by God.

The Bible goes on to say that Abraham and Lot "departed from Haran" (12:4). Haran refers to the wasted years of Abraham's life. He didn't get out of that place until he was seventy-five, when God spoke again. It's as if God said, "Listen up! It's time for you to finish your journey and move on to Canaan, the land I promised your dad."

As I read those words again, I was struck by the words, "Get out of your country" (verse 1). God made it even more emphatic by telling Abraham to get away from the family and from his father's house. He made a number of promises, but nothing was going to happen until Abraham left Haran.

I think of Haran as the place of wasted years simply because it was never intended to be the place God wanted Abraham to stay. The title of Charlie Nelms's book, *Start Where You Find Yourself*, says it well.

That was the message to Abraham. That's the message to you.

Start right now.

Start right here.

Start.

If you're like many of us, you're always trying to plan and get somewhere, but you've never established where you are. Until you know where you are, you're not ready to move on. By that, I mean you need a serious self-examination.

- Where are you?

- Who are you?

- What do you truly want from your life?

- Where do you want to end up?

I have a friend who had a lot of musical ability and an excellent, untrained voice. He often talked about getting voice training. He talked and talked about what a difference it would make to him and to his singing ministry in his local church and that he could go out and minister in many places. He talked about a full-time ministry of singing the praises to God across the country.

One day someone offered to pay for lessons, and my friend turned him down. He finally said, "I searched my heart and realized I didn't really want to learn to be a finely trained singer. I only wanted to talk about it." He said he liked music but he didn't love music. He was content to stay in his home church and sing occasionally.

That's all right. He learned something about himself. He learned what he didn't want. After he had spent a long time looking into his own heart, he finally faced the fact that he had been in Haran for a long time. He had wasted his years and his time. Now he was ready to move into Canaan. He decided to be a certified public accountant (and he has been successful since he received that training).

As I tell this, I'm sorry to say that not all of us are equal. You didn't start equal and you're not at the same place as those around you. If you try to start from where your friend is or the place of somebody you read about, you'll get messed up. That's not where you are. Find out where you are and then get out of Haran!

You'll never get strategic and move into a plan of life until you first answer, "Where am I?" Assess yourself. "Where am I now? What is my true situation? What are my assets and possibilities? What are my liabilities?"

That's how I started to grow. Someone asked me that big question. When I heard the question, I was confused.

"I don't know," I said truthfully, "but I'll find out."

That question sent me on a search to know who I was and where I was. That single question raised many issues in my life. "When I die, will it matter that I was ever born?" That was an implied part of the question. "Am I doing more in my life than just taking up space?" I asked. "Where am I right now? Is this the place to stay or to move on?"

I was in the business world and I knew that was Haran for me. And that understanding led me to another question: "If Haran isn't where I belong, where do I go?" Abraham went to Canaan because that was his destiny. "Where is my Canaan?"

The person who asked me that question was Caesar Clarke, a pastor in Houston, Texas. No one had ever asked me that question before, but I'm thankful he asked. His question truly changed my life.

That question forced me to figure out exactly where I was. I didn't have everything positive going on. My financial situation was in the red. I was running fast because I was trying to finish seminary. I was also working a full-time job. On top of that, I was going through a divorce and that took a heavy emotional toll in my life. With the death of that marriage, I wondered if my dreams would also die. Would God still lead me? Were the promises of God still mine?

"Where am I?" I had to know my starting place. It wasn't a very good place either. But I moved out of Haran and hurried toward Canaan. I want to share this with you because you may be one of those people who hasn't asked that question. You're alone and you don't like being alone. You probably don't like to face yourself and it's not easy to examine your life and think about your wasted years.

You walk into your house or apartment and there's no one else there. Silence meets you and you turn on music or TV just to have noise around you. If you have enough noise you don't have to think. You don't have to look inward. In those moments of silence, however, is the time you're pushed to find out exactly where you are.

Where are you in life? If you cannot assess where you really are in life you can't move forward. Right now, do you feel desperate? That happens when bills are overdue, you need dental work, the kids need clothes, the rent will be due in a week, and you have no money. Your company has talked about downsizing and that might mean you'll be jobless.

I often hear such stories. They're sad and I don't want to take them lightly. The problem is that I hear most of those sad stories from the same people. When they tell me their unfortunate tales they usually say, "I've got to change. I can't keep going this way. I've got to stop this destructiveness and be productive. I'm wasting my time. Every week it keeps going on and Satan walks all over me as time ticks on."

"You were supposed to have fixed that last week," your wife says.

"You said you'd stop spending all that money," your husband says.

"You said I could buy new clothes," your child says.

"You said you'd pay the rent today," your landlord says.

Time clicks by so fast. You're twenty years old and you're going to have a wonderful life and it will be better than your parents ever had.

Tick . . . tick . . . tick.

You're thirty and you haven't gotten any further in your life. You wonder if life is as good as it's supposed to be.

Tick . . . tick . . . tick.

You're thirty-five-years old and you're so busy trying to pay your bills you don't have time to live. You know you ought to cut back on your spending, but you see those powerful ads on TV and you know you just have to have those products. You're bombarded with at least three hundred ads every day. You watch the ads and dial up the 800 numbers and you buy. Your family may be angry, but business-people love you. They love you because you want to buy everything they tell you that you need.

Where are you? When will you figure that out? When will you leave Haran?

Sometimes people call life the rat race and it must feel that way: Rats run through a maze. They don't know where they're going.

They keep on pushing down the maze because they have to keep on running. They're not even sure why they run, but they don't know how to stop.

What's the answer?

Easy. You're not a rat. You don't have to run mindlessly down one hallway to another.

Take one minute—take 60 seconds—and disengage from the world. Think about the things I've written in this book. I'd like you to complete the Strategic Life Plan. I'd like you to focus on it. I'd like you to embrace the teachings. I'd like you to e-mail me and say, "The SLP changed me. I was able to leave Haran and now I'm living in Canaan."

That plan *can save your life*. By faithfully working the plan, you can not only change *your* life, but you can influence and help others. The plan guides you to get yourself together. It's not too late to change. It's only too late if you don't stop for 60 seconds and make the right decision to change.

On a Saturday night, a teenager in our congregation called me and said, "I know you're preparing to preach tomorrow but—"

"But what?"

"I'm working out my Strategic Life Plan and I've got some questions I need you to answer so I can get my life in God's order."

Yes, I was busy, and yes, I didn't like being called on a Saturday night. But yes, those words encouraged me. It was a young person and he wanted to change his life. I was ready to listen all evening. And as I listened, I asked myself: *If I had written a plan when I was seventeen or eighteen, how far would I be right now?*

Despite my late start in asking the right questions, God has blessed me more than I ever thought possible. But I still wonder if I hadn't wasted so many years at Haran, where would I be now?

I'm writing this near the end of the year. Christmas and New Year's will soon be here. People around me talk about the New Year. We drag ourselves through twelve months and as the year comes toward a close we try to get excited about the new one. Too often we don't finish strong in the old one. A lot of times we don't know what we accomplished that year because we never wrote a plan. How can we know if we've made progress?

This is the only answer I can offer: *God expects measurable progress in a reasonable amount of time.*

How do you know if you've made progress? Gone backward? The only way I know to answer is for you to have something written and something to which you can go back and read when needed. Think of it as a contract with yourself. When you have it written, you can measure where you are and where you're going.

I feel strongly about the Strategic Life Plan. I want everyone in our church, and everyone who reads this book, to work on a plan that's so specific you can mark your progress as you move forward every month. Every day you can stay focused because you have a plan to follow and you're not running through the maze with no idea where you're going. That way, you'll also live every day to the fullness of God.

You can prosper if you have a plan. If you don't have a plan, you'll probably fail.

It takes only 60 seconds for you to decide to start a plan for your life. I don't mean a plan to become a believer or to change your ways. That's only part of the plan. I mean a total, all-encompassing plan for the rest of your days here on this planet.

Here is my philosophy, which was stated earlier in this chapter: Everybody ends up somewhere; few people end up somewhere on purpose. The growth of New Birth Church centers on the Strategic Life Plan. We have proven through the lives of thousands of our members that the plan works.

We have taught from the beginning a simple message: You can prosper when you have a plan.

60 SECONDS TO THINK

1. Where are you now?

2. Where is Canaan in your life? What is one significant thing you want to achieve? Make it small and attainable. It can be as simple as saving five dollars from each paycheck. You could commit yourself to reading one chapter each day from your Bible. Such simple steps take you in the right direction. Eventually you can take larger steps.

3. When will you start with the plan? Focus on that question for 60 seconds or longer until you can say, "I'll start now."

4. God expects measurable progress in a reasonable amount of time. Take 60 seconds before you answer this: What is one thing you want to change in your life—one thing you can do in a measurable amount of time and can show a measurable progress? Write your answer.

5. Post your answer someplace where you're forced to look at it every day. For example, you could tape it to your bathroom mirror. Read it every day for three weeks. (Experts say it takes about three weeks to firmly establish a habit.)

12

Accountability

I don't think I need to be accountable to anyone," he said to me. "I can walk with Jesus as well as anyone else. I don't need someone else telling me what to do all the time. If I have the Holy Spirit to guide me, why do I need anyone else?"

"That's a good question," I said. "I'm also sorry you don't have a job."

He stared at me because both of us knew he had a good job. He's in what we call "middle management." "You crazy? Of course I have a job."

"And how long have you had it?"

"Is your mind gone today? I've been there nine years."

"You're not accountable to anyone, are you? You can do anything you want and it's all right?"

I saw the light go on in his eyes, but he wasn't ready to surrender. "That's different. I'm paid to—"

"Yes, but you're still accountable to those over you, right?"

He nodded.

"That's how accountability works. It's not that someone tells you what to do all the time. Does someone follow you to make sure you do what your job says you'll do?"

"No," he said. "As long as I do my job, no one troubles me."

"Exactly right," I said. "That's accountability. But suppose you didn't do a few things your supervisor expected of you. What would happen?"

"I'd get a warning. If he had to warn me a second time, it would go into my record."

"And a third time?"

"I'd have to find a new job."

"That's also accountability. Your supervisor doesn't want you to fail, but he doesn't want the company to fail either. If you do your job, everything is fine. You're a hardworking, conscientious person. If you didn't have to report to anyone, then—?"

He didn't let me finish the question. He got it. He said he resisted finding someone to whom he was accountable because he thought it would be someone who constantly told him what to do. After we talked some more, he was able to see that even if he was accountable to someone, he was the one who set the standard for his own behavior. He eventually found someone he could trust that he could be accountable to, and he told the accountability partner what he would do or wouldn't do. When they met at the next agreed-on time, his responsibility was to say that he had done what he said or that he had failed.

So many people seem to resist the idea of accountability, just as my friend did. They read the Bible and yet they don't get it. Even though the Roman government sometimes persecuted believers, Paul admonished, "Let every soul be subject to the governing authorities. For there is no authority except from God, and the authorities that exist are appointed by God" (Romans 13:1). The same principle is throughout the Bible.

You are accountable to someone in every area of your life, whether it's at work, at school, or in your relationships with others. But many people don't want to be accountable. They like to be renegades. I've even seen this among pastors of large churches. They want to be the first and final word and never take counsel or make themselves accountable. I'm convinced one reason so many people in the public, such as singers, musicians, and athletes, get messed up is because they feel they can do as they please and don't have to be accountable to anyone else. Not only do they make a mess of their lives—and that's just as true for average people—but they miss so many of God's blessings.

I believe strongly in making ourselves accountable. Call it counseling or guidance or whatever you want, but you and I need someone else in our lives to whom we give account.

I'm not immune. No one is. A lot of people have tried to turn me and twist me up because I pastor somewhere between twenty-five and thirty thousand members. Instead of pushing aside others, I realize how much I need. I like to say it this way: My spiritual father is Bishop T. D. Jakes. We pastor about the same number of people, although his membership is probably larger. That's not the point. The point is that I've submitted to him.

I make myself accountable to T. D. Jakes. I could consider myself equal, and we *are* peers. It's not whether he's above me or beside me. I chose to make myself accountable to him. I find comfort and encouragement in these words of Paul. "You must have the same attitude that Christ Jesus had. Though he was God, he did not think of equality with God as something to cling to. Instead, he gave up his divine privileges; he took the humble position of a slave and was born as a human being. When he appeared in human form, he humbled himself in obedience to God and died a criminal's death on a cross" (Philippians 2:5–8, NLT).

Isn't that amazing? Jesus could have considered himself equal to God but no, he humbled himself and did everything in obedience to God. I take that example for myself. If Jesus made himself accountable to our Heavenly Father, doesn't that make it clear that all of us need accountability? I don't have to submit to Bishop Jakes, but I've chosen to do that. I felt that I needed somebody who could put me in check, somebody I would listen to and respect. I needed someone whose word I could respect. I wanted a man who had wisdom and could point out things about myself that I couldn't see (or didn't want to see).

I could have said, "I don't need this, I'm bigger than most of the other pastors and bishops. I have more members under me than they do." I could have kept saying those things, but it's not the biblical way. It's not who has the most members or the highest-paid job. It's that I needed someone who is wise, who cares about me, and who is willing to say, "You are wrong," when I need to hear those words. I voluntarily submit to him for counsel and I let him know any major decisions I consider that have anything to do with New Birth Church or even my personal life.

And that's the thing you have to do in accountability: You have to give permission for someone to be involved in your personal life and your personal decisions. You're still responsible for your actions and you're the one who has to answer to God. But if you have the right person to whom you're accountable, you'll find the decisions are easier to make because you listened. They don't dictate. They suggest, advise, or even confirm your decision. You need an outside voice.

If for no other reason, here's a good one to have someone else advise you. Jeremiah put it this way: "The heart is deceitful above all things, And desperately wicked; Who can know it? I, the Lord, search the heart, I test the mind . . ." (Jeremiah 17:9–10a). Without the counsel of someone else, it's easy to go astray. Because of the wickedness of our hearts, it's a big temptation to make choices to benefit ourselves even if they hurt someone else.

It is always good to have someone look over your shoulder every once in a while and ask you: "How are you doing with this? You said you were going to spend more time with your wife, but you're not doing that. You said you were going to get some more rest, but you're still not getting enough sleep." Someone needs to put you in check.

Ask someone to be your accountability partner. Get help from someone to remind you and to hold you accountable because time and intentions can get away from you. Otherwise, you've moved on (or fallen backward) and you don't even know if you're where you're supposed to be. Unless you make yourself accountable, you don't know if you've done what you need to do.

Is that easy? Maybe not. It takes a degree of humility. The last time I checked, humility meant strength under control. When you allow yourself to be accountable, you also allow yourself to make fewer mistakes. You give yourself permission to move forward more quickly. You can do that because you're open. You're vulnerable and transparent.

If you want to know the secret of my life, the greatest secret of why I've been successful, it is because I believe God called me to success. But I also believe I've attained success because I have opened myself up in relationship to be accountable. Self-humbling keeps me a student. That's also the definition of a disciple. Being a disciple means being open to reality, being open to face yourself and to accept deserved criticism and to be guided by someone who can see the path more clearly than you can. They can see the path because they're not blinded by your desires and self-centered goals. (Remember: The heart is deceitful and you need someone to point out those self-deceptions.)

How do you find someone? It's probably easier than you think. Look at the people in your life. Who are the individuals you most respect? Who do you know that will be honest with you and still love you?

Cecil Murphey was a pastor and part-time volunteer chaplain at a hospital. He became friendly with Jim, another volunteer pastor. One day Jim approached him. "Would you meet with me and make me accountable to you?"

Jim said that he got so busy working for God, he seemed to have no time for God. "I've been careless in praying and reading the Bible. I need someone to help me."

"But why me?" Cecil asked.

"Because I respect you. I've watched you and I know you're a man of integrity." Jim went on to say, "I wouldn't want to disappoint you and that's why I've asked you. It will be embarrassing and humiliating for me to confess that I didn't do what I promised."

The two agreed on mutual accountability. They met almost every week for the next eight years until Jim became pastor of an out-of-state church. Cecil says it was his first experience of accountability to another person. "I've always been fairly self-disciplined," he said, "but Jim pushed me to take spiritual self-discipline even further."

Cec could always tell when Jim failed (which wasn't often). As soon as they met, Jim would try to focus the conversation on other things. Cec learned quickly to say, "Let's talk about accountability first. We can discuss those things later."

They stayed on topic and both men grew in the process.

That's the fruit of accountability. It's fruit all of us need to produce.

You want someone who can see things about you that you may not be able to see, but you need someone who truly cares about you. You don't need a person to put you down or to make you feel weak. That person must be someone who is secure, who is secure in themselves, secure in their calling.

There will be certain opportunities and things that will come your way. If you progress and are successful the wrong person may feel jealous and may even begin to work against you.

Accountability does not mean that a person is lord over you and you've turned your whole life over to someone else to make decisions. To do that would make you a slave and it means you would have released your power into somebody else's hands. For some, turning their life over to someone else works and they fall into the servant-ruler mentality. That's the strength of cults. The followers let their leaders make decisions for them. That means they don't have to think for themselves or figure out what to do. The leaders have all the power and others need only to follow. That's not only a form of brainwashing, but it makes the followers mentally and spiritually lazy. Their actions say, "I'm going to let you decide for me instead of growing and struggling myself."

Accountability simply means you listen openly to the counsel and wisdom of another. Your responsibility is to listen *and* to weigh the opinion of that person. That person may be the voice of the Holy Spirit that speaks to you. Or the other person may be wrong. You need to listen openly and decide whether to obey.

I want to say this straight: *Every Christian needs an accountability partner.* You need to talk to somebody regularly. This is serious business. Without an accountability partner, you'll set yourself up to fail, regardless of your 60-second decisions.

This is a biblical concept. The Old Testament prophet Amos wrote, "Can two walk together, unless they are agreed?" (Amos 3:3). Solomon wrote, "Two are better than one, Because they have a good reward for their labor. For if they fall, one will lift up his companion. But woe to him who is alone when he falls, For he has no one to help him up. Again, if two lie down together, they will keep warm; But how can one be warm alone? Though one may be overpowered by another, two can withstand him. And a threefold cord is not quickly broken" (Ecclesiastes 4:9–12).

Jesus sent his disciples out by twos. "After these things the Lord appointed seventy others also, and sent them two by two before His face into every city and place where He Himself was about to go" (Luke 10:1).

The principle seems clear. You need other people. Nowhere in the Bible is there a case for Christians to be alone or to walk alone.

God has always intended for you to have your arms out to help others, and to have others' arms reach out to you.

If you decide to follow the Strategic Life Plan, don't try to do it alone. Perhaps you can do it on your own. But what if you had someone there to encourage you? To correct you? To help you see where you're weak? Wouldn't it make it easier to have someone who could help you, someone who could make it a little easier for you?

Do it today. Choose someone. Ask for help—and be open when someone asks you for help. Swap e-mail addresses. Exchange cell numbers. Make a covenant with one another that you're going to stay on each other to make sure that whatever you promise gets done.

If you don't do *everything* you promised, you need someone to make you acknowledge that you must face the consequences of your actions or your lack of action. But if you have an accountability partner and faithfully fulfill every promise you make, you'll enjoy a wonderful life.

But even more wonderful than what you attain in life is the blessing on your children's children. You are setting up the plan for those who follow you. You can change your destiny from a failed life into one with a marvelous outlook. At the same time you become an example for the children yet to be born. They'll see you as a powerful, living example of the person God ordained you to be. And you'll have set a pattern of changing and switching lifestyles and patterns of thought.

Ask someone you trust. Paul wrote, "Rejoice with those who rejoice, and weep with those who weep" (Romans 12:15). That's the kind of person you want. You want someone who can enjoy your success with you, and you also need someone who can feel your hurt when you fail or when things go wrong in your life.

You need a person who can *compassionately* push you back to the plan when you fail. Make sure the person is a true friend. A true friend will tell you when you mess up. An honest friend will tell you when you're trying to deceive yourself. A faithful friend will say something like this, "You haven't done anything yet about where you're going. You promised to _____. I'll keep on you every day until you get it done."

Aren't you tired of going from crisis to crisis to crisis to crisis? Aren't you tired of worrying and fretting over your life? Aren't you tired of trying to make decisions and feeling inadequate?

An interesting note in the early history of the church occurs in Acts 16. The leading prophets and teachers came to the city of Antioch where they prayed and fasted, determined to do nothing until they received guidance. During the time they prayed and fasted, "the Holy Spirit said, 'Now separate to Me Barnabas and Saul [Paul] for the work to which I have called them.' Then, having fasted and prayed, and laid hands on them, they sent them away" (Acts 13:2b–3). Again, God didn't send out one person but always someone else to walk by his side.

After the first journey, Paul and Barnabas had differences and Paul chose Silas (he didn't go alone) and went out. Barnabas chose his nephew John Mark and they went in another direction. Always by twos, never alone. In fact, Paul and others apparently had several people with them. They were those they trusted and who would confront them when they needed it.

Because it's such a biblical principle, I urge you to do the same thing. Find a partner. Get someone to work with you on the SLP. Ask a close friend or ask someone you don't know well but whom you highly respect. Ask someone whose opinion of you is important and someone you don't want to disappoint. Don't be hasty, but don't procrastinate. You need to start this serious journey but you need someone to walk beside you as you take the journey.

To ask someone to make you accountable may be difficult. The more difficult it feels probably indicates how badly you need it. If there were no other reason just being accountable could humble you and remind you that you need other people. God never made you to stand by yourself. If you are part of the body of Christ, as the Bible says you are, it means you are connected to other Christians.

You need a companion on your journey. You need someone to hold your hand when you're tired and to hug you when you're discouraged. There are those who need the warm touch and embrace from you as well.

60 SECONDS TO THINK

Here are a few suggestions to help you take that next, significant step.

1. Take 60 seconds to agree with yourself that you need someone with whom to be accountable. This may be the hardest part of the SLP plan, but don't skip it. Don't try to make it alone.

2. Decide how often you will meet. Once a week is best.

3. When you meet for accountability, start out right to the point. Start with these words: "This week, I . . ."

4. Strive for perfection. Don't commit to anything you can't reasonably expect to accomplish. Forgive yourself if you fail. You do that by saying to your accountability partner, "I am sorry I didn't do what I promised. Next week, I will . . ."

5. Take that 60-second pause before you promise yourself in the presence of your accountability partner and state exactly what you will accomplish before you meet again.

13

60 SECONDS TO

Redeem the Time

You've probably had an evil day. Yesterday wasn't so good either. Tomorrow will also be evil unless you make that 60-second decision to change it into a good day.

The apostle Paul says it this way: "See then that you walk circumspectly, not as fools but as wise, redeeming the time, because the days are evil. Therefore do not be unwise, but understand what the will of the Lord is" (Ephesians 5:15–17).

It comes down to this: If you're not using your time the way God has ordained, you have had an evil day. If you spent last week just getting by with no direction, no plan, and no enthusiasm, or if you let other people make decisions for you—if any of those statements fit you—you have had an evil week.

Your week was wasted.

Does this sound like you? You've been nice this week. You didn't steal from anybody. You didn't commit adultery or engage in fornication. If you look over your life for the past week, you can say, "I didn't do anything seriously wrong."

To do nothing wrong isn't enough. The Bible says, "Therefore, to him who knows to do good and does not do it, to him it is sin" (James 4:17). God wants you to do more than refrain from doing bad; God wants you to be actively good. God expects us and commands us to do good. We're to redeem the time.

I'll make my point in another direction. Last night I got home, I went into my wife's prayer closet and I started to read her Bible, which was opened to Ecclesiastes. Solomon had all the money, honor, prestige anyone could want and more than three hundred wives. But he wrote, "'Everything is meaningless,' says the Teacher, 'completely meaningless!'" (Ecclesiastes 1:2, NLT). Solomon had it all—but he also wasted his life. After his death, the nation split and ten of the twelve tribes deserted the once-powerful kingdom. Solomon not only spoiled it for himself, but he wrongly influenced the people of his generation and especially his own children.

What if he had been like his father, David? What if he had put God and godliness first? What if he had made his life count for the good of others instead of only for his own vanity? What if he had redeemed his time on earth? We can't know the answer, but we can say that despite his brilliant and wise mind, he was a failure and a disappointment to everyone.

But you are alive now. You have the benefit of knowing Solomon's history. You can take 60 seconds and determine to redeem the time. You don't have to come to the end of your life and say, "It's all meaningless."

Let's look at your life and the way you spend time. Most of us waste more time than we realize. If you're an average American, you probably spend about forty-five minutes each workday in traffic. And what do you do with that time? How do you fill your mind during that almost hour-long drive? You could do many things to redeem the time—to make that commute time meaningful and spiritually enriching. You could:

- listen to the Bible on CD.

- memorize Bible verses.

- play gospel music.

- hear inspirational books read on tape.

- learn a language.

Think about that last suggestion. You could learn a new language. Why not? We live in a culture where more Spanish-speaking people are coming into this country. They are fast becoming the largest minority in the United States and many among them don't learn English. Even if they do, you can be sure they would appreciate it if you speak to them in their native tongue. You need to minister to them. The most effective way to reach them and anyone else is through language—their own language.

They have to learn English to survive and thrive, but you want them to be able to celebrate in your culture and to feel accepted. You can be one of the first to reach out to them and welcome them into your culture. You can celebrate together and exchange cultures. However, if they already know the language or are learning it, wouldn't it be worth a little time each day for you to learn to speak

Spanish? You could effectively reach out to Latinos by spending that daily commute in learning to speak the language of their hearts. If you take those 60 seconds to make a decision to learn a language, think of the good you could accomplish. You can help others to have a richer, fuller life in this country.

Besides that, how marketable do you think you can become if those forty-five minutes in traffic are spent studying *Teach Yourself Spanish?* If you listen and learn five days a week, three-quarters of an hour each time, by the end of the year you could become bilingual. Learn a new language and you have just valued your minutes, you've redeemed the time, and you've made progress in a changing workforce.

Immediately, I think of a woman named Edith who had a job as a secretary. Her boss was Hispanic. After two months, she realized that more than half of the customers spoke Spanish. She bought a course, listened to it every day to and from work. As she learned to speak, she practiced talking at work. When any of the customers corrected her pronunciation, she endeared herself by saying, "Please say it for me slowly so that I get it correct the next time." Sometimes she used the wrong word and she made each one who corrected her feel good by her profuse appreciation.

Edith started with simple conversational Spanish and progressed only as she felt more at ease. At the end of eleven months, she had become fully bilingual. "I worked hard, and for months I'd translate inside my head. When the day came that I no longer had to go from Spanish to English to Spanish in conversation, I knew I had learned the language."

Because of her language skills, Edith became head of her department within two years.

"If you have the kind of commitment to learn a new language," her boss said, "you deserve to move ahead in your job."

It can be done! You can do it.

That's just one example, but think of the things you could learn while you sit each day in traffic. Make the time useful. If a foreign language isn't for you, buy a course on finances instead of listening to meaningless talk radio. Start educating yourself and don't allow the idle minutes of your day to stay idle. Make those minutes count.

"Redeem the time," Paul urged. There are several things you need to do before you can fully redeem the time.

First, you need to know your assignment. You need to know what you're meant to accomplish. Or another way to put it is this: What's your goal? If you redeem the time, how will you be different? How will you help others?

Here's a biblical example. The apostle Paul went into a synagogue at a place called Antioch of Pisidia and preached a powerful sermon. (See Acts 13.) In the middle of his message he spoke of King David and said, "For David, after he had served his own generation by the will of God, fell asleep, was buried with his fathers ..." (verse 36). The apostle wants to make it clear that King David knew his responsibilities and he realized what he was supposed to do. *And he did it.* "He ... served his own generation." What greater commendation could there be? Because he faithfully redeemed the time, Paul could make that statement about him.

To redeem the time, you must know the urgency. You need to realize not only that you matter to God but the way you spend your time matters as well. Think about Jesus praying in the Garden of Gethsemane. He didn't have two weeks to sit and stare at the surroundings. He had to make a decision and make it quickly because the soldiers were on the way. You need to settle things now. You need to make choices. In fact, when you won't make choices, you have already decided by default.

Some of you may procrastinate or put it off, and that seldom works. You still have to make the decision one day. Why not make it now?

Jesus made His decision after praying several minutes, perhaps even hours. He struggled but He finished his prayer with these words, "Father, if it is Your will, take this cup away from Me; nevertheless, not My will, but Yours, be done" (Luke 22:42). *Nevertheless.* That was the crucial word.

If you're not sure how God wants you to redeem your time and the direction you're to go, here's one way to handle that. Look at where you are and where you think you want to go. As with Jesus' example, you say to God, "I have plans to make a lot of money. Nevertheless . . ." "I want to be the CEO of a megacompany. Nevertheless . . ."

Make the prayer from your heart and listen for the answer. Once you surrender your will to God, you can begin to redeem the time by redeeming your energies. Life works for you instead of against you. You focus your energy on doing the things you know you need to do and that are productive.

At New Birth Church, we have several members who held outstanding jobs in other parts of the country, but they quit those jobs and came to live in the Atlanta area so they could be near New Birth Church. We didn't urge or beg them to come. They came to us because they prayed, "Nevertheless," and listened to what God wanted them to do.

I think of one family that had a lot of money, lived in a ten-bedroom mansion and had a different car to drive every weekday. But God gifted them to work in a place in Africa with raw sewage on the ground, water problems, HIV, and other infectious diseases. Because they were able to say, "Nevertheless," they went to Africa. That's where they use their gifts. They sought God's will and in seeking God's will, they now redeem their time.

When I ponder this topic, one verse has stayed with me a long time. Psalm 90:12 reads, "So teach us to number our days, That we may gain a heart of wisdom." Place that verse alongside Proverbs 22:29, and you have the formula for a balanced, redeemed life: "Do you see a man who excels in his work? He will stand before kings; He will not stand before unknown men." In other words, when individuals do excellent work or work well, they are brought into the presence of those with power.

I've put two verses before you. What do those two Bible verses mean to you?

I hope you get a simple message for yourself: *Don't waste your minutes.* Every ticking moment is important.

That's why you need to know when to go to bed and how much rest to get. In another chapter I write about sleep, but I want to make my point here: You mess up your number of days by not resting when you're supposed to rest. Or you mess up your days when you're supposed to be working but you're resting. You either rest too much and don't work enough or you work too much and don't rest enough. There has to be a balance if you're going to redeem the time and make the most of your life.

How do you balance your life and redeem your days? You need God's wisdom. That's the message of Psalm 90:12: "So teach us to number our days, That we may gain a heart of wisdom." It's a prayer to ask God to teach us. You can't be spiritual and be tired; you can't be tired and be spiritual. There has to be a balance.

When I talk about redeeming the time, I hear a few voices cry out, "How can I do that? I can't get a job."

"Really?" I ask.

"Well, not the kind of job I want."

It's not true that you can't get a job. It may not be the dream job or the job you think you deserve, but you can find work. You can make yourself marketable. When you're marketable, folks want to come after you.

"Do you see a man who excels in his work? He will stand before kings."

Here's one example. A friend told me he had gone to one of those chain restaurants in Atlanta. A young waiter immediately came to their table. Throughout the meal, my friend watched him. The waiter seemed aware of everyone. One thing my friend commented on was that the young waiter cleared tables that weren't in his section. Before my friend could look around for someone to fill his cup, the young server headed toward him with a coffeepot.

"Do you like your job?" my friend asked.

"Yes, sir," he said, "and I like the people, too."

Just before my friend left the restaurant, he asked the waiter why he worked as a waiter. "You seem to have a lot of ability. You're quick. Friendly."

"The company I worked for after I graduated from college merged and later downsized. They eliminated our entire department." A few more questions revealed that he had a business degree, had gone to work as a computer programmer and in three years had risen to middle management. He said he had his application in for several places and hoped one of them would open up for him. "But in the meantime, I like doing this," he said. "I'm with people and I like that better than sitting alone in my apartment."

"And you're doing a good job."

The young man smiled. "I'm giving extra value. My parents taught me to do more than what employers pay me to do."

My friend handed the waiter a business card. "At our company, we're always looking for good talent."

The young man read the card and smiled. "As a matter of fact, sir, I had an interview with your company yesterday."

"Did you get the job?"

"They said they'd let me know." He was off with his coffeepot to serve another table.

A week later my friend visited the restaurant, didn't see the young man, and asked the cashier. "Oh, you must mean Rich. Best waiter I've ever seen. He had several job offers and has become sales manager of some software company."

"I'm not surprised," my friend said and wished he had gotten back sooner.

Every situation may not end like Rich's did, but every person who works to redeem the time—the time *now*—has great potential. One of the best things Rich did was to focus on his present job. For a man like Rich, it was a lowly job, but it was honest work.

Did he dream about the future? Probably, but he focused on the present. He made the most of what he had now.

We can see this biblical principle in a story Jesus told about three men who received large sums of money to invest while their master left for a trip. After the master returned, he called in all three and asked them to give account of the way they had invested the funds. Two of them had invested the money wisely. To both of those two wise servants, the master said, "Well done, good and faithful servant; you were faithful over a few things, I will make you ruler over many things" (Matthew 25:21). The other servant didn't "redeem" the money. He said he was afraid and hid it. For him, the master had nothing but scorn and said, "You wicked and lazy servant" (verse 26).

Two men redeemed the time by using their gifts, their energy, and their time. The story isn't to emphasize who had the most at the start or who came up with the highest amount on the day of accounting. The story is a practical one that says, "Whatever you have, use it. That's why God gave it to you."

Take the account of Jacob's favorite son, Joseph. He may have been spoiled by his father, but when faced with the hardships of life, his real character came out. He could have sulked and thought about what he didn't have and how unfair life had been that his own brothers sold him into slavery. He could have railed at God for throwing him into such a situation. We read nothing like that.

Joseph gave himself to help and serve. He worked his way to become the top servant in the house of a man named Potiphar, who was captain of the guards. Despite the false accusations of Potiphar's wife, Joseph maintained his integrity, worked hard, and stayed faithful. He operated in wisdom to the point that he was later brought into the presence of Pharaoh and made the prime minister. Only Pharaoh himself had more authority than Joseph. That was quite a trip from slavery to rulership. God placed Joseph into the high position and he had the authority over the land because he had prepared himself. He redeemed the time. He did what he could when it didn't seem to mean much. He didn't wait until he was able to do big things.

"Whatever your hand finds to do, do it with your might; for there is no work or device or knowledge or wisdom in the grave where you are going" (Ecclesiastes 9:10). That sounds a little pessimistic, but it means you need to grab everything now and enjoy it now. When you're dead, it's too late.

In one section of the book *My Name Is Asher Lev*, Asher is on a walk with his father. They see a dead bird on the curb. The incident reads like this:

> "Why did it die?"
> "Everything that lives must die."
> "Everything?"
> "Yes."
> "You, too, Papa? And Mama?"
> "Yes."
> "And me?"
> "Yes," he said. Then he added in Yiddish, "But may it be only after you live a long and good life, my Asher."
> I couldn't grasp it. I forced myself to look at the bird. Everything alive would one day be as still as that bird?
> "Why?" I asked.

"That's the way the Ribbono Shel Olom [Master of the Universe] made His world, Asher."

"Why?"

"So life would be precious, Asher. Something that is yours forever is never precious."*

That little incident captures the heart of the command to redeem the time. Nothing is forever. Opportunities come and they leave quickly. Once missed, they're gone. That makes everything we do important, doesn't it?

Look at yourself and look at those around you. The reason many haven't been thrust into the presence of power is because they haven't redeemed the time—they haven't developed the skills to make it worthwhile to be put in that area. They say, "That's not my job."

Years ago I read the true story about a firm that interviewed several people for a high-level position. I remember only the test. The personnel manager dropped a crumpled piece of paper on the floor—but not directly in the person's pathway. When the applicants came in, they couldn't help but see the paper, even though it was small. Without acting as if he noticed, the manager watched to see how many applicants picked up the paper. He said he had used the technique many times before and only about 20 percent of the people who came in picked it up.

If he picked up the paper, the manager asked, "Why did you do that? It's not your job."

---

* *My Name Is Asher Lev* by Chaim Potok, New York: Ballantine Books, copyright 1972, page 156.

He received several answers, but the one he liked best came from an applicant who said, "No, it's not, but it's somebody's job and I can make it easier for that person."

That's redeeming the time. That's making yourself useful and helpful to the world around you—even in such a small thing as picking up a piece of paper.

God says not to waste your minutes. If you're wasting your minutes you're not sharpening your skills. And if you're not sharpening your skills, what would qualify you to be put in front of somebody who has power when you don't even know what you need the power for?

You need a genuine encounter with God and He tells you who you are. When you find out who you are and what you're supposed to do, it's still going to take more than you. Don't be afraid when God actually gives you a vision or burdens you with something because it's so big you know you can't do it on your own or in your lifetime. That's the reason you need to increase your skill and make yourself so sharp in that area so God will hook you up with bankers, financiers, and investors. He'll hook you up with good lawyers and put you in the right places.

You'll be like Nehemiah. He had been the king's cupbearer but he had a vision—a burden that wouldn't let him alone. He heard the report of the Jews who had returned to Jerusalem after the exile in Babylon. They "are there in great distress and reproach. The wall of Jerusalem is also broken down, and its gates are burned with fire" (Nehemiah 1:3).

How did he react? ". . . when I heard these words, that I sat down and wept, and mourned for many days; I was fasting and praying before the God of heaven" (verse 4).

Later when Nehemiah served the daily wine to King Arta-xerxes, we read: "Now I had never been sad in his presence before. Therefore the king said to me, 'Why is your face sad, since you are not sick? This is nothing but sorrow of heart'" (Nehemiah 2:1–2).

Nehemiah told the king of his burden and the king commissioned him to go to Israel and rebuild the walls of Jerusalem. Until that time, he had been *only a cupbearer*. A lowly servant. Who was he to think that he could do that great (and dangerous) work for God? He redeemed the time. He made himself available and followed God's leading. He received the king's permission, provisions of supplies and enough workers, and he went to Jerusalem. Despite opposition from the local heathens, he got the job done.

And you can, too. God will touch the heart of the king and write you a letter of permission and give you favor. When you're skilled and are willing to use your skills, you receive favor. When you're skilled, when you work on your training, you will be used.

Take Denzel Washington as an example. He doesn't just show up and read a script. He prepares for it. He works hard and learns everything he can about the role he is going to play. First he won an Academy Award as a supporting actor. That wasn't enough. He kept at it. He worked at his craft. He made himself available and finally won the award as a lead actor.

Tiger Woods didn't spend his time playing with the children his age when he was small. He got up at four in the morning and worked on his swing until breakfast, went to school, came home, and golfed some more. Now everybody is saying he's lucky or he's just gifted. The boy worked hard and while everybody else was asleep or playing, he was golfing. Now he's getting his return. His minutes are valuable and if you want to sit with him you got to pay for it because he paid up front.

On April 20, 2008, Danica Patrick became the first woman to win an IndyCar Series race, and only the second woman to win any event in the top tier of American motor sports. She was quoted on TV as saying, "It's a long time coming, finally."

You can be sure that she didn't spend her teen years watching boys drive cars. She learned to drive early and it was her passion to win. She was twenty-six years old when she won. She redeemed her time when she was younger and it paid off down the road.

I want to tell you my story that made me realize the importance of redeeming the time. Before I became a pastor, I worked as a salesman for Honeywell. The entire state of Georgia was my territory. One day I drove along I-75 from Valdosta, which is almost to the Florida state line, on my way to Atlanta. As I drove north, on the southbound side a state trooper chased a car. The blue light flashed and the other driver was not going to stop. There was a lot of commotion and cars pulled over to the side. The chased car crossed over the median and was heading south in the northbound lanes.

I saw him as he drove toward me with a state trooper chasing. I looked to my right to try to move over but a U-Haul truck was next to me. While I tried to figure out how to move over and off on the right shoulder, I didn't see that there was any way I could avoid the car hitting me. I pushed the brake, swerved over into the right lane, barely behind the U-Haul truck.

The chased car pushed forward and barely missed me. But it

didn't miss the car behind me. From my rearview mirror I watched as it hit. The vehicles crashed and threw bodies across the road. The driver of the car that was struck died instantly.

I pulled on to the shoulder, turned off my engine, and sat there. If I had acted a millisecond later, I could have been inside the car that was hit. I could have died that day on the highway. I was that close to death. Not only was I thankful that I wasn't hit, but as I calmed my shaking hands, I knew God had a purpose for me, some special purpose. I had to redeem my time on earth to do that job, whatever it was. I had what many would call a wake-up call.

What I want people to see is that all of us are facing a head-on collision with death and non-redemption. But when you cry, "*Abba,* Father," God steps into the pathway of death, grabs you out of the pit of hell, and puts you on the road of life. You need to pull over on the side of the road and thank Him for life. But also thank Him with a sense of urgency that says, "I've got to do something with my life. You saved me for a purpose, God."

When I was a kid we used to sing a beautiful old hymn by Charles Wesley that starts like this:

A charge to keep I have.

I especially like the second stanza:

To serve the present age,
My calling to fulfill:
O may it all my powers engage
To do my Master's will!

That's the sense of urgency you need, and "may it all my powers engage." You need to realize Paul's words, "And you He made alive, who were dead in trespasses and sins, in which you once walked according to the course of this world . . ." (Ephesians 2:1–2a). This means that if you are a Christian, your life is no longer yours. It belongs to Christ. When you were dead, He brought you life. When you staggered in the darkness, He pulled you into the light.

Paul also says in Romans 12:2, "And do not be conformed to this world, but be transformed by the renewing of your mind, that you may prove what is that good and acceptable and perfect will of God." You can't prove the perfect, acceptable will of God if your mind is conformed to this world. Only as you give yourself, do you learn.

Once again from the book of Habakkuk I want to lay down some more practical things. The prophet wrote, "I will stand my watch And set myself on the rampart, And watch to see what He will say to me, And what I will answer when I am corrected" (Habakkuk 2:1).

You are not an accident. Like the prophet, you've been put here to redeem the time and to watch to see what God will say to you.

I have a sign in my office that reminds me of that fact. The sign reads: "I am not an accident. I have purpose and there's a reason I am here in this time."

You're not an afterthought because God had you in mind before the creation of the world. Paul wrote to the Ephesians, "He chose us in Him before the foundation of the world" (Ephesians 1:4).

Here's a tremendous thought: You weren't just a random thought in God's mind. God thought about you before creation. God thought about you before He created Adam and Eve and before Moses and David were born. He also writes about choosing us: ". . . that we should be holy and without blame . . ." (verse 4). When you fulfill your Strategic Life Plan, you're also living a life that is holy and blameless.

Consider this marvelous thought: In the mind of God you had already been prepared for life on this earth before He created the world. If God created you and if God has a plan for your life, you can also rest assured that nothing—absolutely nothing—can hinder you from fulfilling that plan if you start at the watchtower. Go where Habakkuk went. Paul also promised, "And I am certain that God, who began the good work within you, will continue his work until it is finally finished on the day when Christ Jesus returns" (Philippians 1:6, NLT).

You have a purpose. I know I was called by God to solve a problem at this time in the world through Jesus Christ's help. Habakkuk 2:1 says," . . . what I will answer *when I am corrected.*" Please notice the words I've put in italics. Correction, not punishment, is God's way to speak to us and to teach us.

These are strong words: "Write the vision And make it plain on tablets, That he may run who reads it." That is a command; it is not an option. Put that alongside Ephesians 5:14: "Awake, you who sleep, Arise from the dead, And Christ will give you light."

This is the message: Wake up. Be alive. You were asleep (that is, spiritually dead), but now you are alive. For you today, the message is clear: If you don't have a plan, you're asleep. If you have no direction and you don't know who you are and whose you are, you're still asleep. "So be careful how you live. Don't live like fools, but like those who are wise. Make the most of every opportunity in these evil days. Don't act thoughtlessly, but understand what the Lord wants you to do" (Ephesians 5:15–17, NLT).

This is your message: You must redeem the time. If you will take only 60 seconds—one minute—to redeem the time, to make the most of every opportunity, you can change the course of your life.

Too many of the younger generation observe you and me and realize that we don't redeem the time. We waste it. We throw it away. And we're killing them because they have no examples showing them how to use time wisely. The only people they see who seem as if they're prospering are those who don't walk in the will of God. So they think that going to the evil day is the model for behavior. I write that to shame all of us.

God has ordained you and me to change the world around us. To do that, you first have to change yourself and then you can affect your culture. It is the kingdom culture that will affect other cultures, that will draw them in to you so that you are able to show them the true light and the way of life.

60 SECONDS TO THINK

1. I made the statement that you have a purpose in this life. I pointed out that you were part of the plan of God before the world began. In what way are you aware of that purpose?

2. For 60 seconds reflect on this question: What do I need to do so that I can say I truly redeem the time?

3. Write the name of one person you admire, someone of whom you can say, "That person redeems the time." Write the reason for that choice.

4. I've used the word *destiny* in this book. What do you understand this word to mean in your life?

5. Think of one thing that hinders you from redeeming the time. What is it? What must you do to overcome it?

14

60 SECONDS TO

Change Your Thoughts

Think about your daily routine. What do you do at the end of the day? You probably drag yourself into bed. You feel worn out and defeated and how do you pray? It is probably something like this: "Lord, have mercy."

And you need mercy. You're depressed because you didn't get everything finished that you planned to accomplish. You're angry because you know the paycheck you'll get Friday isn't enough to pay all your bills.

But you know what? Those were the same feelings you had last Friday. It was the same thing two years ago Friday. It was the same thing five years ago. You have changed nothing in your life. Okay, that's not true. You're probably more beaten up, more discouraged, and more defeated. Despite all your feelings, however, you haven't made any progress. You're now five years older, living to pay your bills and worrying about what you have to manipulate to have any dollars left at the end.

Let's go back and think about the word of the prophet Habakkuk again. He wrote, "The vision is yet for an appointed time; But at the end it will speak, and it will not lie" (Habakkuk 2:3).

He means there is a predesigned time for God to move you onward. And you can tell you're getting closer and walking with Him because you're being with Him and hanging with the right people. You're at the right church. You also say, "This is where I'm supposed to be. I'm at the right address. I have developed a plan for my family, and I'm seeing my children following God." You know those words and you trust them. God has something for you "for an appointed time." And it will speak at the end.

Habakkuk wisely added, "This vision is for a future time. It describes the end, and it will be fulfilled. If it seems slow in coming, wait patiently, for it will surely take place. It will not be delayed" (verse 2:3, NLT).

There is no magic here. No instant success. You might have to wait for quite a while in your watchtower. But it will happen. It will happen because God has promised. Even if you get discouraged while you wait, remember this: God won't lie. Whatever God reveals to you on the inside, it's not a lie. It *shall* happen. And it will take place in time, a time that's according to God's timetable.

I remember talking to a couple who felt God had called them to Ecuador as missionaries. They applied to a mission board and before they received a response, they quit their jobs and had a FOR SALE sign up in front of their house. "God called us to South America," they said. "We're ready to go."

"But is God ready?" I asked.

They stared at me as if I were out of my mind. As we talked, however, they admitted something: They knew God's guidance for them, but they didn't know the timing. As a matter of fact, more than two years passed before they heard from the mission board and were approved. *Two years.* It might have been ten years. But when the answer came, it was God's appointed time.

That's an example of the way God works. That's why the prophet says to wait for it. It will happen. It will happen because God has promised. When it's the Divine time, nothing can stop it.

It doesn't matter what it is: God has a timetable and He won't be hurried and He won't be hindered. It will work as He chose. But you have to wait for the timing. ". . . it will surely come, It will not tarry" (Habakkuk 2:3).

If you faithfully follow God's plan *and* God's timing, it will happen. Others will see it happen and some will probably say, "You're lucky." They won't understand because they don't expect it to happen to them. They'll have no idea of the time you've spent in your watchtower. They don't see how much midnight oil you've burned. They don't know how you had to go through a period to discipline yourself. They don't know how you had to change your lifestyle. They don't know how early you get up to bless God and how you continue to bless Him. They don't realize to how many people you've sown seeds of love and kindness. They don't realize how many folk you've helped. They don't realize the number of people for whom you've stood in a gap. They don't realize that you had an authentic encounter with God to the point that you read what God wrote in your heart.

This isn't luck. This is Divine order.

This Divine order works if you follow the directions of the prophet and remember that the righteous—the justified—will live by their faith. Because you believe, and because you hold on even when others laugh, your vision will come true. You will see the things God has promised you.

You will have the faith that what God said to you will definitely come to pass. Because you know that, you can say with deep, inner certainty, "I'm going to equip myself in every way possible. I'm going to faithfully follow my plan."

God's plan for you isn't hindered by your divorce; it's not hindered by your lack of education; it's not held back by anything that happened to you yesterday or last year. No matter what your past, you can still fulfill God's plan for you.

"I never went to college," someone said to me recently. "I don't know how I can do the things God wants me to do."

"If it bothers you that much," I said, "you can do one of two things. One, you can go to college. Even if you don't choose college, there is no limit to what you can do with your passion for education. The other thing you can do is support or start a college fund for all those folk who can't afford a higher education. Make college affordable for others by giving your money and you'll see that your name goes down in history as great. You become somebody who never attended college but created the great opportunity for others."

I want you to do strategic planning, but don't limit yourself. Don't think of a plan that lasts for a year or even two. When you do strategic planning it needs to be a plan that will last a hundred years. When you set a plan you need to consider at least three generations. The Bible says that a good man leaves an inheritance to his children's children.

Albert Einstein once stated, "We can't solve a problem by using the same kind of thinking we used when we created it." But if you listen to God, you can find new ways to look at old problems. When you do that you also set the course for generations to come. That is the reason you have to quiet yourself. Get away from the noise and distractions of life.

If you take this lightly and think it is not going to be a struggle, you'll fail. It will be a struggle, because it's not meant to be easy. You have to reach the place where you say, "I'm sick and tired of every year being where I am right now. I believe that God ordained me to have more." When you can say that with conviction, you're ready to change. That's the attitude that will make the difference.

God planted you in America to accumulate resources to help others, not to just make a better life for yourself. You are blessed so you can be a blessing to others. You can bless the brothers and sisters in Africa and India and many other countries. You can bless them all around the world with a strategic plan.

I see a limited focus by many Christians. The other day I spotted a big article in the paper about a church that paid off their mortgage. That's good, but as I read the rest of the article I couldn't see that they had a vision for anything else. At least there was nothing to show that their claim to fame was beyond paying off their mortgage. They did it before their building rotted. And when the building finally rots, they will have to build another one. So what they've done all of their ministry is pay for a building. Maybe they've done more than that, but the newspaper didn't say so. I know a few people in that congregation and I have never heard of any great vision. It's sad that they focus their thoughts on a building. There are so many more important things to consider.

Daniel 4:3 states, "His kingdom is an everlasting kingdom, And His dominion is from generation to generation." If you do not think, operate, write, and give generationally you will not have dominion. He made us in His image and He said, "Dominate." When God identifies Himself how does He dominate? He says, "I am the God of Abraham, the God of Isaac, and the God of Jacob" (Matthew 22:32). He tells us that His strategic plan goes from generation to generation. If you don't understand that, you will never have dominion. You can't have dominion. Nobody will stand in line to continue what you started.

Think for 60 seconds about the way God works. It starts with a challenge. It starts with something to overcome. The change begins when you learn to think differently. You get the challenge and you think, *Yes, with God's help I can do that.*

I hope you'll get excited when you face a new challenge. That means you're about to get blessed. You're about to be stretched into something that no eye has yet seen or ear heard. It happens when you refuse to run from a challenge.

That's why you can prosper. You can make prosperity begin to happen once you've made a serious mind shift. That is, once you change your mind from your old way of thinking. You can then say with conviction in your voice, "I can prosper. I don't have to be beaten down by bills and debts. I won't be beaten down!" You change your thinking and declare, "This is a challenge, and it isn't going to stop me. I'm going to move through whatever it is. Every challenge I have, I'll deal with it and I'll discover what's in it for me. And in the end, I will prosper."

It doesn't matter where you are in your life right now. Whether you're dealing with problems or feel you have overwhelming situations, *change your thinking*. Instead of wailing, "Woe is me," start shouting, "I'm blessed and Jesus is going to bless me even more. Jesus gave me a divine assignment to work through these problems. When I come out on the other side, I'm going to be greatly blessed."

Does that sound like something a preacher ought to say? It's more than that. Here's the Word of God from the book of James: "God blesses those who patiently endure testing and temptation. Afterward they will receive the crown of life that God has promised to those who love him" (James 1:12, NLT).

Open your eyes. Stop crying. Stop feeling sorry for yourself. Instead, start saying to yourself, "God wants me to live a life of joy, of greatness, and it begins when I stop looking downward and focus on upward thoughts." There is something in that situation for you, a lesson, a bone of wisdom, some money. Yes, there's something there.

Here's another example. In Genesis 41:33–37 Joseph interprets Pharaoh's dream. "Now therefore, let Pharaoh select a discerning and wise man and set him over the land of Egypt. Let Pharaoh do this, and let him appoint officers over the land, to collect one-fifth of the produce of the land of Egypt in the seven plentiful years. And let them gather all the food of those good years that are coming, and store up grain under the authority of Pharaoh, and let them keep food in the cities. Then that food shall be as a reserve for the land for the seven years of famine which shall be in the land of Egypt, that the land may not perish during the famine."

That's a strategic plan right there. That's how it works.

Joseph thought ahead. During the years of slavery and imprisonment, he changed his mind. He was no longer the tattletale kid his brothers hated. He became the great servant of others and he waited. He waited thirteen years for God to bring about the promise of his family bowing before him. Joseph focused on positive thoughts and healthy living even during his dark days in prison. His thoughts were right and eventually God blessed him and made him second in command in the country of Egypt.

That's greatness.

That's God.

"Surely the LORD GOD does nothing, Unless He reveals His secret to His servants the prophets" (Amos 3:7). That means that if you and I get quiet enough, God will tell us what's coming down the pipe. There are times when God whispers, "Get ready, get ready." He starts to nudge you that you need to pay off a debt. You need to change jobs. You need to invest. Are you listening to the quiet voice of God? He rarely shouts. Why should He? His faithful servants respond to the slightest Divine pressure.

If you have listened to God and have waited for the fulfillment, everything around you may seem to be going wrong or staying bad. People around you get laid off. Others live from paycheck to paycheck. But you can grin. You can do that because you have changed your thinking. You've listened to God and you were ready. Your grin isn't about passing them up in your new car but it is about how you have used strategic planning so that you have prospered and now you can empower others.

I want to talk to you about how you think and lead strategically to alter your mind-set. Think once again about Jacob in his senior years, and his children huddled around him. Instead of being excited, he was sorrowful because everything his children learned they learned during his younger years. They observed him and followed his example. They picked up his bad habits, his supplanting, his lying, and his cheating family members.

It's not that Jacob's situation is all that different from today. Isn't it obvious (and unfortunate) that we don't have many good role models? I don't even know if we have that many women or men in this church who will stand and pull others aside and tell them things like this:

- "Look, baby, you don't do that."

- "Let me help you with this."

- "Let me show you that."

- "You don't want to act that way and be ashamed of yourself. Let me show you a better way."

You need the right kind of role models, the kind who will not only show you how to change the way you live, but also help you change the way you think. You may be judgmental about other people, pessimistic about life, and always convinced that you're going to lose your job. You may be afraid that you're only one weekly paycheck away from being homeless.

Regardless of your fears and your problems, nothing much will change for the better until you change for the better. Your change begins when you change your way of thinking. I want to help you do just that.

Instead of letting your old thoughts control the way you react, as you have in the past, you can change your way of thinking. You can act instead of reacting. You can teach yourself to try new ways. A large amount of research says that when you change your thinking, the chemicals in your brain also change. It's like jacking up your car and pushing it out of the deep rut in the road. You can then drive on a smooth road.

When God sets people free from drugs, one of the ways they stay off drugs is by changing their thinking. Instead of letting their minds dwell on what they can no longer have, they learn to focus on what life now offers.

I think of an elderly man I once visited in his home. He had not been well for months and stayed mostly in his bedroom. After we talked for a short time, he looked out the window and complained, "It's so gray out there. But that's kind of the way I feel."

It had been a bright, sun-filled day, so I walked over to the window. It hadn't been washed for a long time. I wiped away some of the dirt and said, "It's a brighter day now, isn't it?"

He smiled and said, "It all depends on how you look at things, doesn't it?"

He was right. If you want to see the gray, the dirty, the awful, you can do that. Or you can look through eyes of faith and see the brightness of a warm summer day. You can do that by changing your thinking. Don't focus on the bad but concentrate on the good.

One simple measure is to quote Philippians 4:13 whenever you feel your mind taking you onto wrong paths or negative ways of behavior. "I can do all things through Christ who strengthens me." It's true: You can.

Maybe some people don't want to change. I'm going to be honest with you. I have a struggle with people who won't change. And I have to decide what I'm going to do for them—if anything. One big struggle is with the street-sign people. You know, the ones who hold up signs that read: I AM HUNGRY. I WILL WORK FOR FOOD. PLEASE HELP.

They stand at the traffic signal and hold up their signs as soon as the light turns red. Sometimes I see them ahead and pray that the light will be green when I get there or stay green until I make my turn. "Please stay green, stay green, stay green." And today it was red.

Those sign holders have gotten so they know my car. Recently I was three cars back and the guy with the poster spotted my car and he held up his sign above his head so I couldn't help but notice.

He had me. Automatically, I reached into my pocket right then and handed a bill to him when I reached the corner. My problem is this: Am I supposed to give it to them? Am I blessing them or am I cursing them? My thoughts turn to the negative when I see them. Sometimes I feel judgmental. Sometimes I want to yell at them to straighten out their lives. Are they trying to get work or do they really have a problem so they can't get a job?

So I'm guilt tripping because I have passed by some of the sign wavers. Wouldn't it be greater to be able to empower them instead of handing out a few dollars? Wouldn't it be wonderful if the next time I saw that man on the corner, he wasn't there for himself? What if he was on the corner, trying to get a job for the new sign holder?

We need leaders who are so strategic that folks want to follow them. Leaders who reach and influence others so that they attain a certain goal or object. Leaders like Joseph who are able to make decisions that impact the future of others.

The good news is that you can be one of those leaders who others follow. If you will change your way of thinking, your life will be different. You can focus on what's wrong, on how bad your life is, or you can rejoice in what's good and do good.

Here's a little tip from Cecil . . . and he's not the only person to use such a method. When he awakens in the morning, before he gets out of bed, he lies there and counts off a minimum of ten things for which he's genuinely and honestly thankful. He said that in the beginning, some days it was difficult to think of ten things. But it became easier. Now he no longer counts. "So many things fill my mind," he said, "I could lie in bed a long, long time just giving thanks."

He believed that if he could start his thoughts flowing in the right direction when he awakened, he would be better able to control them and focus them positively throughout the rest of the day.

He also realized that he often felt critical about other people. Often he assumed that some people intentionally did things to irritate or offend him. But one day he said, "I didn't *know* that as a fact. I only thought it. So maybe my thoughts were wrong." He decided that even if his thoughts were correct, he did nothing to improve the situation by reacting.

One other thing he did was to try to catch himself before he said something mean or judgmental about someone else. To himself he would say, "I think and speak positive words about others." Whenever he slipped and said something unkind about another or gossiped, he asked forgiveness and reminded himself of Philippians 4:13.

Another approach people use goes like the old song, "Count Your Blessings":

Count your blessings, name them one by one,
Count your blessings, see what God hath done!
Count your blessings, name them one by one,
And it will surprise you what the Lord hath done.

Instead of thinking as you always do, you can change the way you see things. You can reprogram your mind to think differently. Just quoting Philippians 4:13 or Luke 1:37 ("For with God nothing will be impossible"), you can slowly change your thoughts, which changes your attitudes, which changes your behavior.

* * *

What gets you up in the morning is when you can say, "I have great expectations for today." Those same expectations can keep you going.

You've got to look forward to what you want to do today and to what you want to be. That's the first question you've got to ask yourself: "What do I want to be?" You can make that decision, and if you make it, and your partner helps you stay accountable, you can be and do whatever you want.

If you know what you want to be, every day you'll know what you have to do to make it happen. You have to take small steps at first, but they are steps. And once you choose, God will guide you and help you to honor those decisions.

You can say no to the negative impulses. You can say no to the crowd or the friends who want to pull you away from your goals. You can say yes to the good things. You can say yes to the things you truly want. You can say, "I won't miss moments or waste time. I look forward, I now know what my daily tasks are, and now I'm in a current reality."

Then you can say, "I'm walking now in who I really am. Because who I really am is what I do. I don't have to tell you what I do because you can watch me and see what I do." You can also say, "I expect to have a breakthrough today. As a matter of fact, I've got it written on paper and I know it will happen."

God has promised to provide abundantly and above all that you ask or think. Copy these verses on a card and place it where you'll see it often: "Now to Him who is able to do exceedingly abundantly above all that we ask or think, according to the power that works in us, to Him be glory in the church by Christ Jesus to all generations, forever and ever. Amen" (Ephesians 3:20–21). Get excited. Say to yourself, "Whatever I think, whatever I ask, is nothing compared to what God has planned for me."

You also need to remind yourself, "I need to be directed in the right way. I can leave the past behind. I can change. I will change. I am beginning to change right now. Today."

60 SECONDS TO THINK

1. For 60 seconds consider your thoughts. What one negative or wrong thing you've thought recently troubles you most?

2. Count your blessings. Write down ten things for which you're thankful. Ponder another 60 seconds and write down ten more.

3. "I can leave the past behind. I can change. I will change. I am beginning to change right now." Say those words aloud. For 60 seconds ask yourself what you want to change.

4. Spend another 60 seconds and remind yourself of Philippians 4:13 and Luke 1:37.

5. Remind yourself that every time you think in a positive manner, you become spiritually stronger. You get blessed; you bless others. You can change and you can start the mind change right now.

15

Bridge the Gap

I have a dog and he's a trip. I sent him to get trained. He went to a school and after he came back he was good for a few days. But within a week he was back in the past.

That's how it is with us, isn't it? We make a good start, we learn things, we make commitments, but if we're not careful, we fall back into the old ways again—the old paradigm.

Today we use the word *paradigm* a lot. It refers to an example that serves as a pattern or model, especially of a lifestyle or a type of behavior. You form your paradigm by doing the same thing or reacting the same way long enough that it becomes habitual. Once you've established a paradigm it's not easy to change.

Once you decide to change, however, you have to keep yourself in check because of your past paradigm—the way you dealt with people, the way you went after things, and the way you spent your time.

The best way to change the paradigm is to ask yourself the question God asked Moses: "What is in your hand?" That means to examine yourself, to consider your resources. Take inventory of what you have and what you can do. What talents do you have? What experiences?

What is in your hand? What do you have the ability to do? Don't belittle yourself or anything about you. Instead, figure out what you can do.

For you to do that and to change your paradigm, you must bridge the gap between seemingly opposing principles. And there are several gaps you have to face.

In this chapter I want to talk about bridging the gaps. *Gap one refers to the old ways of functioning and the requirements of the current reality.* Take the matter of time. Under the old paradigm, you had a few minutes of extra time and what did you do? You dialed on your cell. You thought of three people you had to talk to right at that minute.

If you change your paradigm you won't use up your monthly minutes and they'll roll over. Even better, you'll spend your time on activities and things that will make you a better person, someone more useful to God's kingdom.

The issue is change. You know you need to change, but you need to be aware of something. You need to consider the consequences. Ask yourself, "What happens if I change?"

For one thing, change brings criticism. You'll find out who your friends are and you'll learn those who aren't your friends. I guarantee you if you start making a dynamic change your friends are going to criticize you. "You used to be one of us," they'll say. "You think you've become too good for us?"

That's how it happens. Think of John the Baptist. He was that wild man who wore animal-hair clothes and ate locusts and wild honey. His father, Zacharias, was a priest. And because he was the son of the priest, everyone expected John to follow the traditional pattern of doing what his father did. But John didn't. I'm sure they jawed his daddy: "Why doesn't your boy wear a robe and stand inside the temple? I saw him out on the street talking about repenting and telling people to change their ways. Who does he think he is?"

But there was John, doing his thing by introducing repentance and preparing the way for God to send the Savior. He was in the right, despite what others said. He was moving in what God had ordained and everybody else was talking about him because he wasn't in church with his robe. He was standing in the gap for others and pleading for them to change their ways.

God isn't looking for a bunch of people to come to church; God is looking for you to *be the church* and get yourself where you can upset folk and cause them to criticize you because you stand in the gap, and you stand for the right way. A crooked stick doesn't know what to do with a straight stick. You live in a nation where few people are straight enough for them to see the right pattern. But God called you to change your paradigm and let it be a witness to others. And God will give you all the help you need.

Another consequence is that you'll actually like yourself better. You'll appreciate yourself more because you're not following the trail everyone around you follows. You'll discover new roads to travel and you'll like the ride and enjoy your life a lot more.

One further consequence is that you'll develop a new circle of friends. You'll attract people who encourage each other. They'll also be people who want to stand in the gap and make life better for others.

Gap two is that there's a space between your vision and your present circumstances. It's the difference between what you see now and how you want things to be. The result is a challenge to the status quo. You can decrease that gap every day until you fully eliminate it.

Let's go back to young Joseph. He had a dream. He saw years earlier that sometime in the future his father and brothers would bow to him. None of them liked his dream and they told him to shut up.

Joseph had to grow up and he did. Eventually he challenged the status quo and the gap between his present and his future disappeared. He couldn't do anything while he remained the young dreamer, but he knew what lay ahead. His then-present circumstance led him to get thrown into a pit.

Despite all the troubles and problems, Joseph never forgot his vision. People were mad at him because his dream transcended the status quo. Status quo is when someone looks at you and asks, "Who do you think you are? Who are you to change things around here?" And you know who you are and you know God has called you to make those changes. They may get upset at you the way Joseph's brothers did, but you need to hold on to your vision.

Are you still not sure that's true? Okay, I'll give you a good way to check out your true friends. Talk to them about your dreams. Tell them where you intend to go (and mean it). That kind of talk trips folk out, because when you are confident that you're going to get there, your excitement scares them. They don't have a plan and they have no dreams that they work toward. Because they're scared, they don't want anyone else to succeed either. If you all stay down, then they don't feel so bad. But if you pull ahead of the others and change your life, they also feel guilty. They don't like that either.

You might be in a pit today and, like Joseph, you might be in jail tomorrow, but if you're faithful to your vision, after it's all said and done, God will show you favor. You'll be the one to rule. People may be mad at you but God won't be. You can count on this: God will bless you and you'll be the one who triumphs and rules.

Gap three refers to the future. It's about expectations. I talked about past paradigms and establishing new ideas and ways of thinking. The issue involves learning and means you don't stop learning. The issue is not just learning information or getting degrees, but stretching your mind, your understanding, and your abilities. It's moving beyond the people around you, not because you feel superior, but because you refuse to let them hold you back. "I have a destiny," you have to say. "I have a purpose. That destiny and purpose doesn't allow me to get pushed along with the crowd."

It's easy to follow the crowd and it takes effort to pull away from them. It doesn't matter whether you're in school or in the workplace, people run in packs. They follow someone else and the easier it is to follow, the larger the crowds. It doesn't take any effort or any thinking on your part to follow someone else. Not many people want to think for themselves. It's even harder to find those who stand up for themselves, especially when everyone else seems to go in the opposite direction.

But suppose you ask:

- "What if?"

- "Why not?"

- "Is there a better way?"

- "Why do you want to do that?"

- "Why can't things be different?"

- "Why can't life be different?"

If you ask such questions, you'll get answers and all of them will encourage you to get out of following others. You'll make your own way and others will follow you.

To stand in the gap and separate yourself from the pack means you want to learn, to stretch, to move beyond what is now. It means you want a better way. You're tired of hearing people say, "That's the way it has been and that's the way it is, and that's the way it will always be." But you're not only open to stretch, you've grown restless. You don't want to look, talk, and act like everyone else. You have a vision and you're ready to move out even if you have to do it all alone.

"There's got to be something different," you say. "It's got to be better." And it will be if you stand in the gap and follow your dream.

I'll tell you about a woman who challenged the status quo of her day. She was an African-American woman named Madam C. J. Walker. Her challenge to the status quo began when she found it difficult to comb her hair. "There's got to be a better way," she said. "My hair isn't like white folks' hair. It has a stronger curl." She thought about the situation for a few days before she bought a metal comb and it wouldn't work.

Madam Walker got frustrated and threw the metal comb across the room. It landed on the stove. She started to grab it, but instead she held back. She watched the metal heat. She heard herself say, "Hot comb. Hot comb! That's it."

That's when she invented the hot comb.

Madam Walker was a widow, poor, and worked as a laundress for about a dollar a day. She was careful with her money and somehow she saved enough to educate her daughter. She also became active in St. Paul's African Methodist Episcopal Church in St. Louis. As a member there, she developed her speaking and organizational skills.

She was born in 1867, and by 1917, she owned the largest business in the United States operated by a black person. She said of herself, "I am a woman who came from the cotton fields of the South. From there I was promoted to the washtub. From there I was promoted to the cook kitchen. And from there I promoted myself into the business of manufacturing hair goods and preparations . . . I have built my own factory on my own ground."

She also said, "There is no royal, flower-strewn path to success. And if there is, I have not found it for if I have accomplished anything in life, it is because I have been willing to work hard."

Madam Walker saw her personal wealth not as an end in itself, but a means to help promote and expand economic opportunities for others, especially black people. She took great pride in the profitable employment—an alternative to domestic labor—that her company afforded many thousands of black women who worked as commissioned agents for Walker's company. They could earn from $5 to $15 a day, in an era when unskilled white laborers earned about $11 a week.

Because she said, "There has to be a better way," she invented the hot comb and became the first black woman millionaire.

That's her story. She stood in the gap. She was in the gap long before the comb fell into the fire. Someone else could have seen the same thing but done nothing about it. She was ready and waiting for an opportunity. When a seeming accident happens, God can bring great results when the observers see that as their chance to stand in the gap. Her willingness to think beyond the present was what made the difference.

Her story makes me think of Jesus. When He came, He stretched people and established a new standard with the Sermon on the Mount. He said several times, "You've heard that it was said to those of old . . . but I say to you . . ." (See Matthew chapters 5–7.) It was as if he said, "People tell you to act this way, but I want to tell you a better way." Not everyone listened, but those who did were the people who stretched and lived happier and more fulfilled lives.

Gap four refers to immediate needs and future promises. The issue is choices; the results are rewards. You have to make choices between immediate needs versus waiting for the promises of God and of things to come.

As Habakkuk promised, "It will come, it will not tarry. But it's for an appointed time."

"So something is coming," you say. "That's nice but I have needs now." That's true, but it doesn't mean you ignore the future by being so fully involved in the present. You have a choice. You can blow your plan on trying to satisfy the immediate cry. Or because you know what's coming, you can choose to make a few additional sacrifices through choices to ensure that you stay focused on what God promised you.

I want to tell a story that illustrates my point. Before the contractors laid the carpet in the new auditorium at New Birth Church, we held a special service. We invited people to come and write promises. They were promises to God and to themselves. They were to write them, put them on the floor, and the next day the contractors would lay the carpet over them.

If we were to rip out that carpet right now, we could still see the promises. I wonder how people would respond if they read those words today. I'm sure some of them kept their promises. I'm also sure some of them messed up and joined a generation that no longer stands on their promises.

Some of them left their promises because they were pushed by immediate needs and couldn't look ahead. They came to church for instant gratification and encouragement and were unable to look forward to what God promised. But there were others, the people who said, "I'm going to stand on my promise. I'm going to be faithful to it because it was a promise. I promised myself and I promised God."

But there are always other voices, aren't there? "Yes, I know God is good and honors us," they say. "I want God's best, but right now I have so many other things crowding my life. When things get better or when I have more time or save up a little money, I'll get back to the promise."

They dream, but they're only dreams and can never turn to reality.

I urge you to think differently. You can say, "I don't need a car right now. I'll ride the bus, because when I can get a car I won't be stressed out with how to pay for it. I've made the decision not to get in debt. I'll give to God and put aside what I can and one day I'll have that car. [Or that house or whatever you want.] God will help me because I'm willing to do what I can. I have a plan and I'll follow that plan. I've got a strategy and I know it will work."

This kind of thinking is fruitful because it means you know that if you open your heart to God and if you cooperate by coming up with a plan to realize your dreams, God will make them happen. As you promise God, you also believe that God says, "I've got a plan for you, I've got a destiny for you, I've got a dream for you and only you can fulfill it."

People often quote Jeremiah 29:11, and it's a good promise. Through the prophet God spoke to the Jews in captivity in Babylon. He said He would bring them out of bondage and do great things for them. As you read the promises quoted below, think of yourself as one who has been in captivity. That is, as someone who has been carried along by the crowd and now you're ready for God to deliver and bring you into the Promised Land of fulfillment. I've copied the whole promise, which is Jeremiah 29:10–14:

> For thus says the LORD: After seventy years are completed at Babylon, I will visit you and perform My good word toward you, and cause you to return to this place. For I know the thoughts that I think toward you, says the LORD, thoughts of peace and not of evil, to give you a future and a hope. Then you will call upon Me and go and pray to Me, and I will listen to you. And you will seek Me and find Me, when you search for Me with all your heart. I will be found by you, says the LORD, and I will bring you back from your captivity; I will gather you from all the nations and from all the places where I have driven you, says the LORD, and I will bring you to the place from which I cause you to be carried away captive.

God promises and He will fulfill His word to you. For example, God also promises, "So shall My word be that goes forth from My mouth; It shall not return to Me void, But it shall accomplish what I please, And it shall prosper in the thing for which I sent it" (Isaiah 55:11).

It's as if Jesus puts His arm around your shoulders and says, "I saved humanity in three and a half years walking with My disciples. I'm giving you sixty, seventy, or eighty years. I don't care how old you are, I have a plan for you. But you need to write a strategic plan for the next hundred years. You need to become the most powerful, prosperous believer in the world. You need to start with 60 seconds that lead to greatness."

Some people who read this book will see me before they leave this earth. I expect some to say, "Thank you, Bishop." I also know others will say, "I wish I had listened."

"I wish you had listened, too," I'll have to say to the second group. "There is a time when it is too late." Night comes and the daylight is gone. I often think of the story of Noah. God grew weary with the wickedness of people and said, "My Spirit shall not strive with man forever . . ." (Genesis 6:3a).

God chose Noah and said, "The end of all flesh has come before Me, for the earth is filled with violence through them" (verse 13). He told Noah to make an ark and gave him the dimensions. That man spent a lot of time building an ark and, according to the Bible, there had never been rain before. But he built what God told him and finally Noah and his family went inside. Once they were inside, God closed the door.

We don't know much about the wicked people of Noah's day but I'm sure that if any of them had believed God's solemn promise to destroy the populated earth, they could have joined Noah's family. They had years of opportunity.

Then the door closed.

From then on, it was too late. That's how God works. The secret is to be ready. When Pharaoh needed someone to guide the people during a period of great prosperity, he said, "Find me somebody wise." He sought somebody skillful and wise and he gave his whole kingdom to a man of God. He gave that kingdom to Joseph.

The story of Joseph and his faithfulness reminds us that people will come after you when you tap into the Spirit of God. Perhaps you know the story of Daniel, who was carried away to Babylon. He refused the rich diet of the king and ate simple foods. He prayed. He tapped into God's Spirit. That gave him the ability to read, to understand, to discern, and to interpret what was going on because he remained on the outside. He listened only to God and not to the other voices.

That's something for you to remember: If you're going to stand in the gap, you can't be involved with everything of the world and still tap into the Spirit of God. You need to be in touch with God and open to His Spirit. Early in the book of Revelation, John says, "I was in the Spirit on the Lord's Day" (Revelation 1:10). The apostle had been banished to the isle of Patmos. God took him out of the situation, put him in a remote place, and separated him so John could speak to the situation.

That doesn't mean you need to move into a monastery or become a hermit. It does mean that as you move around in this life and associate with people, they need to know that you're not part of their situations and problems.

If you remain outside their activities and don't become one of them, when you speak they'll hear you because you stand outside, but you don't condemn them. In the Bible, Abraham's nephew, Lot, moved to Sodom, and when it came time for God to destroy the city, the Sodomites didn't want to listen to Lot. He had visitors in his house and tried to shield them from the wicked people.

They scoffed at Lot and said, "This one came in to stay here, and he keeps acting as a judge; now we will deal worse with you than with them" (Genesis 19:9).

Lot's word was useless. He was no better than they were so why should they listen to him? It's just as true today. You have to stand away from the crowd, not with pointing fingers, but stand away so that when you speak, they will listen.

They'll hear you when you speak in your wisdom because God will have given you a revelation of their situation and they will know, even if they're not saved, that there has to be a God because there's no way you would know what you're saying unless He said it to you. They will know you are godly, and they will listen. They may not change, but at least they will listen.

Here is the secret to standing in the gap and being ready: Strategic planning. Write your vision. Make it plain. By contrast, God says, "My people are destroyed for lack of knowledge" (Hosea 4:6). He means they will perish for a lack of information. You're one to bring that knowledge into your community.

You cannot afford to have all kinds of noise around you when there are others who want to get with you, to learn from you, and to move forward. Those noisy folk represent a distraction. They may be nice people and good, wonderful folk. You may need to say, "You're such a nice person, and you're saved. God blessed you and filled you with the Holy Ghost. That's all good news and I've got all eternity to spend with you. But I can't do it now. Right now, I need to redeem my time for the kingdom."

If you have a divine vision of what He has written inside of you, you need to remind yourself of something else: Your vision cannot be completed in your lifetime. That's why it's so overwhelming and that's why God identifies Himself as a generational God. "I am the God of Abraham, the God of Isaac, and the God of Jacob," He says. You are, whether you want to accept it or not, connected to your children and you are connected to your fathers and mothers and forefathers. And in all that, there's something that is to be processed for the kingdom and the plan unfolds and becomes fulfilled.

You are not an independent person standing with just yourself. You influence, you are influenced. That is the reason it is so important to remind yourself that you don't have time to hang with people who are part of the crowd. You need to identify with whom God has already joined you. Find the right crowd to walk with, but make sure they're the people who will uplift and encourage you.

Probably everyone has had an experience where you've met somebody and almost instantly you felt that you were divinely connected to each other. They were going in the same direction as you were. They are out there and they're the kind of people you need to seek. And then you could talk about God and where each one was because God was speaking the same thing to you. God has aligned and raised up people or assigned people at certain times to come into your life.

If you're spiritually discerning, that means you're not anxious and you're not messed up, and you're not worried. You can tell who God has joined you with to help further the kingdom agenda that is in you.

But there's the dangerous side, too. If you start placing a lot of people around you that have not been joined to you, they become placeholders. That's all they are and nothing else. They don't harm you and they don't help you move forward. They just take up space in your life.

I learned in school that a placeholder was a zero. All of you have zeros around you and they block the ones God sent to walk beside you. You cannot afford to have those zeros around you. They block out the God-sent people who want to get with you and walk with you to help you move forward.

As I pointed out earlier, when it came time to build a cathedral, the first generation planted the trees and started the foundations. The second generation worked the walls and the third generation would cut down the trees planted by the first generation, to make the furniture for the cathedral.

That leads to these questions: Are you preparing for the next generation? What have you planted for your grandchildren? For your great-grandchildren? What do your grandchildren have in store for them?

One time I asked that of a woman and she said, "Well, I'm not a grandmama yet."

"Maybe not, but you're going to be one. Whether they're your literal grandchildren or whether they're the children of future generations, your life will impact them."

She didn't answer so I added, "Your daughter is sitting right next to you. Look at her. What have you put in line strategically for her children? For your grandchildren?"

She got it then.

"A good man leaves an inheritance to his children's children," reads Proverbs 13:22. And it's not just an inheritance of money. I write more about this in chapter 19, but it's important to think of what you leave behind when you depart from this world. You can stand in the gap and reach out to those behind you and those in front of you. You can be the force that pulls them together and changes the course of history.

You may not have a dramatic effect on the entire world, but God will use you. Think of the unnamed boy who stood in the gap. He was the difference between people going hungry and leaving with full stomachs. A crowd of more than five thousand people had followed Jesus. None of them had brought food. "One of [Jesus'] disciples, Andrew, Simon Peter's brother, said to Him, 'There is a lad here who has five barley loaves and two small fish, but what are they among so many?'" (John 6:8–9).

From that small lunch, Jesus performed a miracle and fed thousands. That boy stood in the gap. He did what he could. I'm sure he wasn't planning to be part of a miracle. He was there because he had followed the crowd that led him to Jesus.

That boy stood in the gap. He stood where you can stand right now. It may be as simple as sharing your lunch or encouraging a disheartened person. But it begins with a commitment to a plan. It begins when you're ready to stand in the gap and be a servant of Jesus Christ.

60 SECONDS TO THINK

1. For 60 seconds think about yourself. What is one thing you want to change? What will it cost you to make that change? I've asked this in previous chapters, but I ask it again because it's important.

2. Ask yourself, "What happens if I change? How will I be different?"

3. There's a gap between your vision and your present circumstances. It's the difference between what you see now and how you want things to be. Pause for 60 seconds and ask yourself what you want to see.

4. The third gap refers to the future. What do you expect to have in your life? What are you preparing to happen in your life?

5. Identify the placeholders in your life. Plan now to move away from them. Fill your life with those who will help you move forward. Make this a serious and urgent commitment.

16

Increased Faith

You can't make your own faith, but you can reach out for it. You can't manufacture faith, but as you focus on God at work in your life, you can begin to believe more fully. As you increasingly see God's hand in your life, your faith will increase. God tells us to have faith in Him and in His words. Here's what that means.

You must have faith that:

1. God is with you.

2. God is within you.

3. God leads you.

Faith isn't ignoring the facts, and it's not limiting God to the facts. Look at those three things I've mentioned. Do something for me, or even better, do something for yourself. Take 60 seconds and think about each of those three things.

1. Say to yourself, "God, You are with me." I'm sure you can recall several experiences when you sensed God was with you. You sensed His presence. You started to do something and felt some kind of inner check. You weren't sure what to do, but you prayed and an idea came to you. You obeyed and later realized that God had truly led you.

2. Say aloud, "God, You are within me." The New Testament stresses that God's dwelling place or habitat isn't in temples or human-made buildings. We, human beings, are the dwelling places of God. When you opened yourself to God, when you said you wanted to believe and follow, you became God's holy temple.

   Just before the Jewish leaders stoned him, Stephen preached a powerful sermon in which he traced the history of Israel and said that Solomon built a house for God. "However, the Most High does not dwell in temples made with hands, as the prophet says: 'Heaven is My throne, And earth is My footstool. What house will you build for Me? says the LORD'" (Acts 7:48–49).

3. Say, "God leads me." As soon as you speak those words aloud, the temptation is to think of the times you didn't know God led you or you disobeyed His leading. Confess your failures and forget about those times. Think of the times when you knew God directed you. By heeding an inner warning, you avoided an accident. You received a good job because you

prayed and that job just seemed to open to you. Think of at least three times when you *know* the Holy Spirit led you.

One final thought on this: Just because you don't feel all the things you want to feel doesn't make the experience not true. Sometimes children don't feel loved by their parents, but their parents do love them. *The feelings are real but they are not reality.* Even if you don't feel loved by God, the reality is that God truly loves you.

Stop right now and make that 60-second decision.

If it helps, read these words aloud:

God of my salvation and God who loves me, I have chosen to follow You. I have decided that I want You to guide my life and to lead me in every way. Thank You that You are with me and You are within me. Amen.

One major factor holds back many people—and it may be one reason you are held back from greater faith. That reason is fear. If you focus on your fears, you won't grow. Fear fights faith. It's that simple. If you're like Peter and see the tumultuous waves below you, you'll sink. But if you look inward and upward and remind yourself that God is faithful, you can do the seemingly impossible.

In some of my dark times, I think of the words of comfort from Lamentations. Scholars believe the book was written shortly after the fall of Jerusalem and the people were carried away captive. They attribute the book to Jeremiah, who in the midst of pain and loss wrote: "The thought of my suffering and homelessness is bitter beyond words. I will never forget this awful time, as I grieve over my loss. Yet I still dare to hope when I remember this: The faithful love of the LORD never ends! His mercies never cease. Great is his faithfulness; his mercies begin afresh each morning" (Lamentations 3:19–23, NLT).

You believe or you fear. You can't do both at the same time. And most people look at the waves instead of seeing Jesus standing on the waves in front of them. I want to focus on some of those fears.

The number one fear I see among Christians is the fear of the unknown. I don't just mean fear of death and what lies ahead. I mean fear right now, today, in making decisions and in stepping forward. When God encourages you to move you hold back and remember how you failed a dozen times before. Don't do that. "But God," you cry out, "I don't know what's out there. What if life is worse out there than it is now or than it was before?"

I know a man who understood for the first time about paying his tithe. He fully believed that one tenth of his income belonged to God, but he struggled with how he could give that much and stay out of debt. "But God," he moaned, "I can't do that. I can hardly pay my bills now. If I give You a tenth, I'll go into debt. I'll be a bad example to people." For days he argued with himself and with God. But he was also tormented.

About that time he read in the book of Malachi where God promises, "Bring all the tithes into the storehouse, that there may be food in My house, And try Me now in this . . . If I will not open for you the windows of heaven And pour out for you such blessing That there will not be room enough to receive it" (Malachi 3:10).

In desperation, he cried out, "Okay, God, I guess I'm afraid to trust You. You made a promise so I'm going to hold You to it. If

You'll bless me and provide for me if I'll give You one tenth, I'll do even better. I'll give You fifteen percent. Now, let's see You provide."

To his amazement God provided. He had less money than before but it seemed to go further. Two years later he said he was more prosperous than he had ever been. And through the years, he's never given less than 15 percent.

I don't think this is a model for everyone, but I cite this because that man realized his fear and he faced it. He stepped out of the boat and he did not sink.

The number two fear I see among Christians is fear of failure. "But God," you cry out, "I tried that once. It didn't work and I failed. I'm afraid to fail again." I hear that one a lot. I hear it in churches and in other organizations: "We tried it once." Because the program or project failed, they won't try it again.

Please note that God's timepiece is not in sync with yours. Please understand, He isn't on your schedule. Your time frame isn't God's time frame. Your time is always quicker than His. You want it now or tomorrow at the latest. That's not how God works.

Let's say you are about to be evicted. You pray for God to come through and to perform a miracle for you. If God is going to intervene, it must be by Thursday at noon. You pray Tuesday and plead for intervention, but nothing changes. It's Wednesday. "Something's going to happen," you say, "something's going to intervene. Lord, come on." Thursday at twelve you're desperate: "Lord Jesus, please."

At twelve fifteen the sheriff and a truck pull up. "Please, Lord, please don't pass me by."

It's a sad day down at the missions because that's where you end up.

I'm laughing with you but I've also been there. You see, I lost my home and everything I owned. I became homeless and I was sitting there and I thought, "God, I'm following You and doing everything You said. I've got no furniture except a mattress and a radio and my boy has his stereo. We have no music to play. Don't take my house, Lord."

But God took the house. That happened in 1984, and later I stood in front of the house and screamed to anyone who passed by, "I used to live there."

Where was God when I needed Him so badly? I didn't know. Nobody cared, or so I thought. But God did care. I had to go through two years of really hard times, but look where I am now. At the time I lost the house, I thought I had lost everything. I now realize I had lost things—only things—and now I've gained life and success and God has fulfilled my dreams far beyond what I would have thought. I was just in too much of a hurry for God.

I've heard hundreds of stories of people who felt as if God had failed them at a terrible point in their lives, but they held on anyway. Later—and sometimes it was years later—they looked back and said, "I'm grateful for that experience. It turned out to be a greater blessing that God didn't intervene. I didn't understand because I couldn't see ahead. I could only see the present."

I'll give you biblical examples. The prophet-priest Samuel anointed David and said he would become the next king. He did, but it happened thirteen years later and after David was almost killed several times by King Saul.

Joseph made dreams known to his father and brothers when he was seventeen. He was thirty before God fulfilled the dreams and he became a ruler in Egypt.

God tagged Elisha as the heir apparent to Elijah. Elijah told the younger man to stay with him every day and if he was there on the day Elijah left this life, he would be his successor. Elisha waited. He followed and served the prophet until his mentor was swept up in a whirlwind and traveled in a chariot of fire into heaven. The Bible doesn't say, but scholars think it happened many years later.

God promised Paul that he would speak before kings and gentiles. It was years, perhaps as many as twenty-five, before Paul finally stood before a king. In the meantime, despite persecution and imprisonment, that man became the major voice in the early church. He alone wrote two-thirds of the New Testament.

Do you get the picture? God wants to grow your faith. It seems it would be easier for you if miracles transpired every time you prayed. It doesn't work that way. God seems more interested in the longer view. He has things ahead for you that your mind can't possibly conceive. He prepares you for those times by not making it easy now.

In 2007, my cowriter's house burned to the ground. As he stood in the driveway and watched his house burn up, he said to his close friend, "God prepared me for this." He didn't mean he had a premonition or a warning. He meant that he had gone through difficulties and hardships in the past. Each one of those hard times made him stronger and more trusting. Even when he lost all his possessions, he was able to say, "God prepared me for this."

He's no different from the rest of us. God is in the preparing business with you as well. You may not understand a thousand things that happen. You can't grasp why you didn't get that perfect job or why your marriage failed. But God knows things you couldn't possibly understand. He's constantly preparing you for the future.

If you're going to do something significant, God first puts you in the oven and bakes you. As He bakes you, He puts some wisdom into your young self. And He adds a dose of patience. He seasons you well. And when you think you're ready and have gone through enough, you tell God, "Okay, I'm ready. Get me out of this."

You're not ready yet. God has to turn you over and bake you on the other side. The heat never seems to let up. You begin to ask, "Will this ever end?"

Finally, God smiles and takes you out of the oven. "You are ready," He says. Or as Paul writes it, "And let us not grow weary while doing good, for in due season we shall reap if we do not lose heart" (Galatians 6:9).

If you had been able to ask Abraham where he was going, he would have said, "I don't know where I'm going, but I will know when I get there. As soon as God tells me, then I'll know."

The reason Abraham would know the place when he arrived there is because it would be something that God did for him, and he would end up in a place where only God would get the credit. Here's the principle: Wherever you go, it's to bring glory to God and not to make you more important or wealthy. You may become important or influential or wealthy, but that's not the major reason you're in that place. You're there because God put you there. Whatever you achieve, it's because God made it possible.

I've achieved a lot in my life, but I don't want people to praise me. I want them to see that God took a kid who wasn't supposed to be bright enough to go to college, changed his life, and used him. That's what gives praise to God. All of us have known of famous people who were gifted and they acted as if they did it all and even gave themselves the gifts. They're so wrong. And many of those self-important people ended up tragically.

This is God's world. If you want God to smile on you, you must recognize what He has done, what He is doing, and praise Him for all of it.

Here's another illustration from my life. For the first three years after I became a pastor, I preached in Cedartown, Georgia. During those three years and the first four years as pastor of New Birth, I puked before almost every service. I was afraid to speak publicly. I didn't think I was a public speaker and I was afraid I would fail. And I told God regularly, but He wouldn't release me.

Once I overcame my fear of failure, the vomiting stopped.

The number three fear I see is the fear of the impossible. Most of us pray that God will talk to us and tell us what to do and where we're going. We face obstacles that we're sure we can't possibly overcome.

Ever think about Abraham? He was seventy-five years old and had never fathered a child. But God promised, "You'll have a son." That seemed impossible. To compound it, Sarah would be the mother and she was already old. Even more impossible was that from his child, from the promised son, there would grow a great nation so large in numbers no one could count them.

Impossible? Of course it was.

Even so, Abraham believed God, even though he had every reason to believe he could not produce children. He waited twenty-five years. During that period he had questions. And I'm sure he questioned a hundred times whether God had truly spoken to him.

Please note: The fulfillment did not happen in a day. It did not happen in a week. It did not happen in a month. I'm sorry to say, it didn't happen in a year. It took twenty-five years and during those years Abraham had to address all the questions and doubts that constantly troubled him. I'm sure he must have asked himself some questions, such as:

- What if I obey God and nothing happens?

- Have I missed a signal?

- Did I not hear God correctly?

- It's been a long time since I got the promise and I'm still waiting on the manifestation. Will it ever happen?

- Is it possible that an old man can be a father?

Abraham had his doubts. So did I about my calling. My questions weren't the same as his, but they felt that big.

- Has God really called me?

- Does God want me to preach? To be a pastor?

- Why would God want me?

- I have a good career going now and I can witness to people. Why would God want me to give up my good job?

I had question after question and I couldn't answer most of them—at least not then. But I surrendered. I answered the call because I knew God had tagged me to preach. I didn't know where I was going and I didn't know if I would succeed. I didn't know if I could do an adequate job, but I answered the call. Even after I came to New Birth, it was still a long time before I knew I was where I belonged. (I wasn't as smart as Abraham.) Because I answered, God blessed me and through me has blessed many others.

Always remember the God factor: You do what you do because of the ability of God. You do what you do because of the wisdom of God. You do what you do because of the plan of God. When God appears to call you to something impossible—really impossible— the question is not what is impossible to me, but what is possible for God? Luke 1:37 says, "For with God nothing will be impossible."

The fourth fear I see is fear of the future. It is amazing how many know they need to move forward but they won't. "I'm afraid. I don't know what to expect. I don't like my life the way it is, but at least I know what I have to fight against every day. At least my misery is predictable." So you say, "But if you'll just show me, I'll do it."

You can't quite believe that God has a great future for you. You want that great future, but you want the future drawn out for you. You'd like God to tell you everything that's going to happen in your life or at least tell you about the successes you'll have.

Forget it. God shows you only what you need to know now. He will show the future when you need to see it. To see everything isn't faith. To trust God when everything speaks against the future bliss is faith. Faith says, "I don't have any idea what lies ahead. I may be afraid but I know You're with me, You're within me, and You'll lead me."

The real question that comes from the fear of the unknown is how do you handle the absence of facts? Hebrews 11:8 says, "By faith Abraham obeyed when he was called to go out to the place which he would receive as an inheritance. And he went out, not knowing where he was going."

How many people hear God speak one morning and say, "Quit

your job"? The Lord didn't tell Abraham to quit his job, the Lord told Abraham to leave Haran. He was to travel to a place he didn't know. He had absolutely no idea of his future address. He knew only that if he was going to follow God, he would go on a long journey.

He obeyed. He did it. He may have feared the unknown, but he trusted God more than he feared.

Abraham was just one ordinary man. We don't see anything particularly gifted or unusual about him. And yet by his obedient action, he determined what Israel was going to become. Don't take the story of Abraham lightly.

You're not Abraham, but you have no idea what God will do with your life or how the Lord will use you. Your actions will affect a lot of folk. You'll be blessed beyond your expectations if you obey. And if you don't obey, one day you'll have to give an account. You'll have to stand before God and say, "I was afraid of the future. I didn't trust You."

In that moment you'll see the blessed of the world as they file past you. You'll look around and see others—people like yourself— who could have changed the destiny of the world. You'll all stand with bowed heads and your hearts will be filled with shame.

It doesn't have to be that way. Believe. Trust. Trust doesn't ever mean a lack of questions. Trust doesn't mean that you've overcome all doubts. Trust means you're aware of the obstacles, but you believe God more than you believe statistics and facts.

Follow the example of Abraham. He is called the father of faith and his first assignment was to face the fear of the unknown. He didn't have many facts about his destination and God didn't give him any information. That bothers you and me not to know everything. We live in the information age. We have computers and Internet and databases and we find almost anything we want to know. We don't like to go to a strange place without a GPS in our car. You can download data, but you can't download faith. Faith comes from within.

You have to step into the unknown. You might be a little fearful, but keep on. If you wait for enough information, you will never go forward because you'll never get enough information to make it safe and easy. Sometimes in life you will have to go places and do things without knowing what's ahead. You act or you step out because you believe that you're doing the right thing. You do it even if your friends and family think you're crazy.

That's part of the reason we developed the Strategic Life Plan. We want you to look at yourself and, even more important, we want you to look at God. What is God telling you to do? Where is the nudge in your soul that you're afraid to act on? Don't be afraid. Take the next step. We want to help you jump into the unknown and trust God to guide every step. And He will.

When God speaks and doesn't give all the information, the person who goes first is called a leader. If you obey God, at some point you have to pull away from the crowd. If you do, faith will be the deciding factor.

"What is faith?" I hear people asking that question all the time. Here's the biblical answer. It "is the confidence that what we hope for will actually happen; it gives us assurance about things we cannot see" (Hebrews 11:1, NLT). That's the definition: inner assurance and unseen evidence. You have the inner assurance, but you have little outward evidence. To move ahead requires that big step of faith. But if you read the entire chapter of Hebrews 11, you see example after example of godly people who acted on little more than their inner assurances and trust in God's faithfulness. Each section of the chapter begins with two significant words: "By faith . . ."

- By faith Abel offered to God a more excellent sacrifice than his brother (verse 4).

- By faith Enoch was taken away so that he didn't die (verse 5).

- By faith Noah moved with godly fear and built an ark, even though the earth had never had rain before (verse 7).

- By faith Abraham left his home and went out and had no idea where he was going (verse 8).

- By faith Sarah conceived a child in her old age (verse 11).

The list goes on and on all through the history of the godly people of the Old Testament. In every period, there were those who believed God in spite of the evidence—in spite of not knowing the outcome.

So settle it in your heart. When God speaks to you, don't wait until you have all the facts. You'll never get all the information you want, but you'll get enough to know that you need to act. You need to change. Cutting-edge people constantly move into uncharted territory.

God told Abraham to go and he went. He didn't have the written history of God who fulfills His promises, as we do. You can read all about how God faithfully dealt with all those who came before us. So, will you go? Will you do whatever God asks you to do?

Will you pause again, right now? Will you stop and ask God to help you become a spiritual, cutting-edge believer? Will you take one minute and decide to listen to God no matter how foolish, irrelevant, or impossible it may seem?

To make it a little easier, I want to quote this promise: "Trust in the LORD with all your heart; do not depend on your own understanding. Seek his will in all you do, and he will show you which path to take" (Proverbs 3:5–6, NLT). Ask God. Listen for an answer. Act. It's that simple. It's not easy, but it is simple.

I hope you've made that choice. We used to sing, "I'll go where you want me to go, dear Lord." I don't hear that song these days. Too many people want to camp permanently on solid ground and wait for God to come to them and take them into the future. God calls you to obey. To obey requires movement. Action. You have to do something. As you move forward, God meets you.

An excellent example of this is the account of the children of Israel getting ready to cross the Jordan and go into the Promised Land. "And it shall come to pass, as soon as the soles of the feet of the priests who bear the ark of the LORD, the Lord of all the earth, shall rest in the waters of the Jordan, *that* the waters of the Jordan shall be cut off, the waters that come down from upstream, and they shall stand as a heap" (Joshua 3:13).

It happened exactly that way: ". . . and the feet of the priests who bore the ark dipped in the edge of the water (for the Jordan overflows all its banks during the whole time of harvest), that the waters which came down from upstream stood still, and rose in a heap . . ." (verses 15–16).

Too many want another sermon, another confirmation, a voice

from heaven, or an authority figure to tell them what to do. Too many of you are stuck along the banks of the Jordan River. You're waiting on Him to part the water and it's not going to happen.

God says to you, "I'm not parting the water until you step into it. You take the first step and I'll meet you. And if you don't get into the water, you're going to be stuck on the other side of the promise. You'll look at the promise and never be able to see it fulfilled. You'll die on the other side of the Jordan and your children will stay there, following your same paradigm."

Frankly, if God had told me everything that lay ahead of me after July 1987, I don't think I would be where I am today. I might have been too intimidated. I might not have believed Him. At that time, I was a preacher of a small church. God spoke to me as clearly as if I had heard an audible voice telling me to leave the city where I was living. I didn't understand. I had no idea what lay ahead. But I did what God told me. When I moved forward, God moved toward me. The result (so far) has been the 250-acre campus of New Birth Church.

I stepped forward. Are you stepping forward? Standing still means you're not moving and nothing will change until you move.

60 SECONDS TO THINK

1. Take 60 seconds to look at yourself. Ask yourself, "What holds me back from trusting? What holds me back from believing God's promises?"

2. Finish this statement: "If I trusted God to be with me, I would . . ."

3. Read again about the fears that fight faith. Which is the most powerful fear in your life? How can you combat that fear?

4. Here's something to do for yourself: Don't only take 60 seconds right now to ask for increased faith, but pray for it each day. Set aside just one minute and ask. But if you ask, make certain you're willing to follow whatever God asks you to do.

5. Faith grows. As you respond in faith to little things in your life, God increases your trust. What is one small thing you can do that shows you are willing to believe God and to move forward?

17

Eliminate Distractions

There are a lot of things I'd like to have. I've seen the advertisements for the American Dream, but I have to admit to myself that the American Dream hasn't anything to do with the kingdom of God. All things you see advertised on the road signs, in the magazines, on the Internet, and on TV are a matrix kind of thing. It's a kind of worldly subculture; it has nothing to do with God.

Despite the ads and the way they pull you to dream of bigger, better, and newer, it's also a trap. For you, as a believer, it's like Egypt was for the Israelites—it's the place to keep you imprisoned. It's the place to keep you in bondage. It's difficult today not to get caught up with such things as ads for the better life, and they cleverly enchant you to yearn for them, even if you don't need them.

From a spiritual point of view, they distract you. They often make you want things you would not have ordinarily considered or thought about. But worse, they keep you focused on things that don't last and hold you back from learning and growing. All around you are words, noise, and information.

Think about some of those ads. They want you to talk about the most popular hip-hop, the latest football scores, the newest bling, and the sleekest car models. They distract our children. For example, while teachers explain algebra, the kids are text messaging each other. They spend more time reading text messages than reading their English text.

The kids are wrong, but part of the fault lies with their parents. Too many parents haven't learned to "redeem the time." Maybe you're one of them. You have not taught yourself to redeem the time and you haven't taught your kids either. You have not asked them what they put into their minds. Take that iPod out of their heads and put in something that's going to stretch them and move them toward godliness. Once you finish with that then maybe you can use some leisure time to listen to something that you have judged good enough to go into your spirit.

I want to make this point: Your ear canal is your life's birth canal. That is, whatever you hear and conceive inside your mind, you work out through your thoughts and actions. The more you put into your ear that has nothing to do with God, the more you become distracted from spiritual things. Distraction leads to destruction of your spiritual growth. To behave like a disciple of Jesus, you have to know who Jesus was (and is) and what He wants His followers to do.

There is no way you can listen to the world every day and come to church on Sunday and think you're going to walk close to God. You don't get credit because you showed up on time. Your presence on Sunday doesn't impress God. He wants you to show up every day able to learn so you can bless and teach.

If you're like the people around you, you waste your time. That's what most of them do. They're not out doing a lot of evil things, but they're not doing a lot of good things either. They're so distracted they don't have any time or energy left for God.

You've been having real evil days, not walking in wisdom, not walking in knowledge, not even going after the good things. And if you're not careful, you're also hating on everybody who is successful. "If they look like they're doing it right," I heard someone say, "they've got to be doing something wrong." If that's the way you think, your mind is warped.

Successful people feed themselves successful, positive things. Their minutes are maximized. They started somewhere with that 60-second decision to eliminate distractions and learn to focus on what is important in life. But too many of us don't get it.

Not long ago, the University of California at Berkley released a study that said the average person encounters more than three hundred advertisements in the course of a single day. If that's true, think of the implications of that. Every day, three hundred voices tell you what you want, what you need and must have, what to do with your life today, and they'll even tell you what will make you happy, who you ought to become, and who you ought to be with. They know what's sexy, and what's worth your attention. Or they say they know.

Those three hundred voices keep you busy making choices about things that don't matter. They leave you terminally distracted from the sacred questions of life. If those ads succeed, you don't wrestle with real-life issues.

It's easier to think about bad breath, gray strands of hair, or Preparation H. You don't get it that you're being manipulated, because you're trying to figure out what color is in and which designer jeans are the current style.

Did you know you need to drink Johnny Walker to be cool? How do I know that? I saw it on a billboard. I didn't know where it came from but the ad makes it clear that if a man—any man—can hold a liquor glass, wear a nice suit, and give a big smile, he's successful. Where did I get that message? The same place we get all such messages, and none of those messages are in the Bible.

Nowadays you've got young men growing up and holding liquor glasses because they think that's the way it's supposed to be. Now you've got a whole new generation that judges popularity and success on the latest style of bling, and the more you have and the more you can flash it means you're successful. And if a man can get a half-naked woman to stand next to him, he's got everything going in life.

I could go on and on. Those things attract attention, but they're not what's really important. We live in a sick culture that continues to teach superficial values. Unless we challenge it, we continue to encourage it, and nobody wants to stop it.

It's time for all of us to make a change. It's time for *you* to make a change. It's time for you to take another 60-second break and eliminate all distractions from godliness. Those distractions seem to always be around you, even in church. I know, for instance, that a lot of people sit in church and they're thoughtful enough not to disturb others with a ringing cell phone. But they put their cell phones on vibrate so they won't miss a phone call. Their vibrating calls become more important than God's call. How many calls do you get in a day that won't wait an hour? The cell phone is a minor distraction, and only one of many.

Some distractions, of course, are far more serious. For example, too many people get distracted over sexual sins. But any distraction that pulls us away from God is every bit as dangerous. If anything can stop us from listening to God's word and prevent us from worshiping God, it is a distraction. And if it distracts from what we need to be doing, it is evil. It is sinful.

You and I have become so conformed to electronics that we're hardly aware of the minutes and the hours we throw away and can never reclaim. When we waste our time (and we do that when we have nothing to show for our activities and spent energy), we've failed.

Most of us don't just allow one or two distractions, but many. And once you allow a few minor things to distract your seconds, you also become careless about your minutes. When that happens, your days are evil, too, because now every spare moment you have and your children have you're plugged into an iPod, looking at a video, playing a game, and you never have a moment to sit and meditate. "I'm so busy I can't find time to read my Bible," you say.

It's bad enough for you to allow distractions into your life. It's worse because you let people who don't know God or care about God tell you how to use your time and energy. They're people without moral values. For you to talk about meditating on God would be a tremendous joke to them.

Too many people, even serious Christians, don't get this. They think it only takes a few minutes to play a video and it's a harmless distraction. I'm not against recreation and don't want the task of telling people what they can and can't do. I want to say instead, "Is this what you think God wants you to do? Is this godly or is it a distraction?"

You don't steal so you think you're all right. I have some bad news for you. God tells you to redeem the time—to make the most of it. You need to fill your minutes with things that count, with the things that last to eternity. If you don't, you are stealing. You're stealing the seconds and the minutes of time (and of life) that God entrusted to your care.

In Romans 12:2, God asks you to prove what is good, perfect, and acceptable, but you cannot do it. He says not to be conformed to this age. That means, you're not to be hooked into its stuff. Please understand a lot of the sin that is going on is because we have conformed to the age. Because those around you (even other believers) do certain things, you're encouraged to do them. But if you do, those little things will drive you spiritually off track. You don't hear God's voice. You *can't* hear God's voice.

When it comes to hearing God, I think of the story of Elijah. He had defeated the prophets of Baal and then, afraid of the wicked Queen Jezebel, he ran away. He hid in a cave, but God knew where he was and God wasn't going to let him be distracted by fear or depression.

1 Kings 19:11–12 reads, "Then He said, 'Go out, and stand on the mountain before the LORD.' And behold, the LORD passed by, and a great and strong wind tore into the mountains and broke the rocks in pieces before the LORD, but the LORD was not in the wind;

and after the wind an earthquake, but the LORD was not in the earthquake; and after the earthquake, a fire, but the LORD was not in the fire; and after the fire a still small voice."

It's not that God wasn't literally in those things, but that Elijah couldn't hear God speak. It was as if the prophet listened for God in all the noisy things of life. They were the distractions. Elijah didn't hear God in the noise or in the earthquake because that's not where God was speaking. He heard God in the place you and all of us can hear: in the stillness. You can listen in the silence. God speaks in the quietness of the heart.

Stories in the New Testament help us understand that Jesus never allowed noises, even loud, terrible ones, to distract Him. I really like the story that's recorded in Luke 8:22–25. Jesus got into a boat with His disciples and told them to cross to the other side of the lake. "And they launched out. But as they sailed, He fell asleep" (verses 22b–23a). While Jesus slept a windstorm came down the lake. "And they were filling with water, and were in jeopardy. And they came to Him and awoke Him, saying, 'Master, Master, we are perishing!'" (verses 23b–24a).

It was a serious moment, at least to the disciples, and they believed their lives were in danger. Jesus obviously wasn't worried. In fact, He was still asleep despite the noise and the shouting. After they awakened Him, He rebuked the wind and the raging of the waters. He didn't speak to the disciples then. He waited until that distraction was gone. When it was quiet once again, He spoke. "Where is your faith?" He asked (verse 25b). In the Gospel of Mark,

He said, "Why are you so fearful? How is it that you have no faith?" (Mark 4:40).

Both accounts end with a reference to the awestruck disciples. They're suddenly afraid of Jesus because He calmed the storm. "And they feared exceedingly, and said to one another, 'Who can this be that even the wind and the sea obey Him?'" (verse 41).

They missed the powerful lesson Jesus wanted them to learn. First, He showed them His absolute trust in God because He slept through the terrible, thunderous noise. Second, He was upset with His disciples because of their lack of faith and rebuked them. They had traveled with Him and seen His miracles, so they should have known. They failed because the storm distracted them. The storm robbed them of their faith. Finally, they focused too much on the miracle and they didn't learn the lesson. They realized that Jesus stilled the storm, but they didn't grasp that He did it to teach them.

It may encourage you to realize that even the people closest to Jesus got distracted. First it was the storm and then it was the miracle. Either way, their gaze left Jesus and fastened on distractions around them. You have your own storms, perhaps daily. Some are possibly life threatening, but most of them would fall into the category of distractions. They keep you from concentrating on what's important at the moment. Here's an example of what I mean. One man I know carries three cell phones. If he sits down to eat with me, he displays all three. "I don't want to miss an important call," he once said to me. He explained that one cell is for friends and family, the second is for office calls, the third is for overseas business calls. And he keeps all three going all the time.

The problem is that he's more concerned about missing a call on one of those three phones than he is about enjoying the company of those who are with him.

Years ago I attended Dr. Robert Schuller's Institute for Successful Church Leadership. He said one thing that hit me then and has stayed with me. "To succeed you must choose your failures."

"That doesn't make much sense to me," I said to him.

"I've failed by choice," he said. He added, "When I don't return your phone calls, that's a choice. When someone says to me, 'You didn't call me back,' I admit, 'You're right, I failed.'"

While I waited for that to sink in, he said, "But I sure preached Sunday, didn't I?"

I smiled because I finally understood. That was Dr. Schuller's way to say that the time he could have spent in returning phone calls he used to study and prepare to preach. For him, phone calls were a distraction. As important as some of them may have been, they would have distracted him from the thing he needed to do right at that moment: study and prepare his message.

I admire Dr. Schuller and we've since become friends. He admits that he doesn't make many appointments and he fails to return calls. But he'll turn right around and tell people about his successes. He has succeeded because he decided where to spend his time. He decided to have more balance in his life and to eliminate the trivial and the less important so he can focus on the totally important.

But the most valuable lesson he taught me was that it's all right to fail to pay attention to distractions. As good as some of those things may be, they're like the fire and the earthquake of Elijah's day. They make noise and have great visual effects, but they're only distractions.

I understand a few things about distractions because of my own experience, and I want to confess to you my struggles. One time I went on an overnight retreat with one of my close friends, and we had invited two others we both knew well. We decided on the retreat because we realized how much we missed each other's company. We liked the fellowship we shared with each other. Besides, both of us needed a break from our heavy schedules.

A few minutes after the four of us met and greeted each other, we decided to eat dinner together. We sat at our table and immediately each one of us pulled out our cell phone and began to return calls or check our e-mail. *All four of us.*

The waitress took our order. That is, she did between the times we talked on the phone. We started to eat and someone's cell rang. Then another's rang. Some of us talked between bites. My cell rang and I, too, began to talk. One of the men turned his back to me and looked out the window while he spoke on his phone.

At one point, I looked around and all four of us had our phones going. We had been together almost an hour but we had spent more time on the phone than we had talking with each other.

This is madness, I thought. I turned off my phone and decided to sit and watch the other three. I didn't say anything. Why should I? Until I turned off my cell I had been as busy as they were. We finally finished dinner and between phone calls—all urgent, of course, or so it seemed—we did talk a little.

The next morning we met for breakfast. The other three pulled out their phones and repeated what they had done the night before. For a long time I didn't say anything, hoping they would notice I wasn't talking on my cell. That didn't work. I cleared my throat and said, "Gentlemen, I need to say something."

"Wait a minute," one of them said. "I saw you sitting there watching us talking away on our cells. I already know what you're going to say."

I spoke anyway. After I talked a minute or two about our cell-controlled lives, a second man said, "Isn't that ridiculous? We come together to get away and we bring our problems with us."

We all laughed. We even told each other a few funny stories about cell phones.

One of them made a shrewd observation when he asked, "Do you realize how many people actually go to dinner with you when you're on your cell?"

We laughed some more, but I think we heard him. "At dinner yesterday, there were at least four people at our table besides us."

"More than that," one person said. "I talked to three different people."

More laughter followed, but after that, when one of us answered his phone at the time we were supposed to be eating, one of us would pull up another chair to the table. That would end the phone conversation.

In the middle of breakfast, my buddy answered the phone. We tried not to listen but he stayed on that call so long we not only pulled up a chair, but we also called the waitress over and ordered for that new person at our table.

When he heard us giving the order, he got off the phone real quick and canceled the order. "I understand," he mumbled.

That was a great lesson for the four of us. I still forget sometimes, but I'm working on it. Here's what that habit says to me:
"You can't break away from your friends or business associates long
enough to bless God. The phone is more important at that moment
than anything else in the world." And that's certainly not how I
want to lead my life.

At church I've seen people duck behind posts or rush out into
the lobby. The worst offenders, of course, are those who sit in church
and text message. I'm sure they hope their neighbor will think
they're taking notes.

What does this say about distractions? It says we're so caught
up in instant communication that we can't disconnect for a moment
to hear from God or to praise God. We have to deal with other
things and allow ourselves to be distracted by the world. I don't say
to avoid those calls, but we need to learn to handle them at the ap-
propriate time.

We've become a generation of addicts. Most of us aren't on
crack, pot, or speed, but we're electronic junkies. So far I haven't
been able to break the habit; I'm constantly distracted. I struggle
but I haven't totally won this battle. *But I will win.*

And you can win, too.

Think about the distractions in your life. Why is it that you have
to go into your house and turn the television on when you don't
plan to watch it? And every room you walk into, you switch on the
lights or the TV. You go downstairs and your children all have iPods
in their ears and they listen to music or play video games. You try
to get their attention but you don't succeed. They're pumping themselves and reprogramming themselves and are distracted by the
noise they hear.

It seems as if no place is immune. When you go to the hospital they've got the TV on in the patients' rooms. I've gone through that situation hundreds of times. I try to talk to my friend or family member and I can't hear them. The TV distracts. And it's not just when they're in the hospital. I've called patients after they've gone home. They answer and I can hear the words from the TV plainly. The person says, "Speak up, Bishop."

"Maybe you need to turn off your radio or your TV so you can hear me," I sometimes have to say. I don't want to shout louder than the crying women on *All My Children*.

I don't know all the reasons we tend to do this, but of one thing I'm sure: We're afraid of silence. Why are we afraid of silence? Again, I can't speak for everyone, but one thing I know: Silence forces you to face things. If you don't have distractions and noise going on around you, you have to think. You examine your life and rethink your previous actions. You might even pray. If you pray you might even hear God.

Silence intimidates.

Silence pushes you to listen to things that go on inside your heart. Often they're the things you may want to avoid. But they're also the things you need to ponder.

Silence means God can speak and you're not sure you want to hear.

How can you hear God when too many other voices crowd out His voice? We work it so we're constantly distracted. You can plug into an iPod, look at a movie, play a video game, or have TVs going on all through the house. The house is noisy, so you decide to leave it and jump in your car. But of course you have to play your CDs or listen to the radio.

You drive to church and after you go inside it's so quiet, you can't stand it.

I know. I've watched this many times. If things get really quiet, I can expect someone to yell out, "Hallelujah!" "Oh, praise God!" I'm not against praising the Lord and saying such things, but sometimes people throw out those words so they can have noise.

Are you like that? Do you have to have distractions? Do you need something to drown out the silence?

That means you avoid the powerful, significant questions that you need to ask regularly:

- Who am I?

- Whose am I?

- What do you want me to do, Lord?

- What do you want me to say?

- What is my destiny?

- How am I displeasing you?

Unless you learn early about the grace of Jesus Christ, you become lost in the sea of utter distractions. You don't hear God when He does speak.

I mentioned the texting back and forth that goes on in church and I'm aware of it. The messages seem so important at the moment. But they go like this:

I left four messages.

Sorry. Busy.

What are you doing now?

Nothing.

Great, insightful moments, aren't they?

If you look back and think about what you've done, you've been successful. Yes, you have because you have successfully wasted a lot of time. One minute on a message doesn't seem long. But one message leads to another and to another.

But what if you used the one minute differently? What if you used those same 60 seconds to get rid of distractions? What if you used that small amount of time to hear God speak?

Your minutes are too noisy and too distracting for God to speak. It's like having too many people sitting at your table. God can't get your attention long enough to communicate.

Or you can think of it biblically: You have conformed to this age. You haven't discerned what Paul means when he writes, "Don't copy the behavior and customs of this world, but let God transform you into a new person by changing the way you think. Then you will learn to know God's will for you, which is good and pleasing and perfect" (Romans 12:2, NLT).

As I wrote the words above, I again confess that I know all about the noise and distractions. I want it to be absolutely clear that I'm guilty. I've been caught up in the distractions as well. Sometimes it takes me hours to get quiet, even when I'm by myself, because I've got all kinds of noises and messages and feelings of guilt and duty. Sometimes the noises in my head have accumulated throughout the day and I have to shake them away. Yet Isaiah promises, "You will keep him in perfect peace, Whose mind is stayed on You, Because he trusts in You" (Isaiah 26:3).

You don't have to allow all those distractions. You can have that perfect peace by turning off the noise. You don't have to answer every e-mail and every telephone call. You don't have to turn on every TV in the house. What's wrong with a few minutes of silence each day?

This is also a place to talk about setting up boundaries. People invade your space only if you allow them to do so. They may not have boundaries but you can set up the no-trespassing signs and refuse to let them distract you. If your friends call you at inappropriate times or call you to intrude on your privacy, it's all right to say, "I can't talk now." Or you can ignore certain calls. It's all right to leave your cell phone in the car when you go worship God. Instead, you need to be on Divine call so that God can get through to you.

If you set limits, your friends may not like it, but they'll respect you for your discipline. They may even test you a couple of times, but if you hold on to your boundaries, they'll learn.

Do you want to have your boundaries? Or do you want people to distract you from spiritual things? For some people, sitting in silence, waiting for God to speak, being open to the Holy Spirit seems almost impossible. They can't shut off the outer noise and if they can't do that, how can they shut off the noises inside their heads?

Cecil was a pastor for several years. On Sunday mornings, he wanted people to pray for others. He did what he called an informal bidding prayer. That is, he mentioned a need, such as the name and condition of a sick member. He paused and waited in silence for people to pray. He discovered that twenty seconds was the *ultimate* limit for silence before paper shuffling, coughing, and movement took place.

Silence isn't easy to achieve in our world. If we tried silence for ten minutes at New Birth Church or any other congregation, for most of the people that might be the most difficult ten minutes in their lives.

Try it at home. Try it right now. Put this book aside and sit without doing anything for ten minutes. Try three minutes. Even one minute can be difficult for some people. If you're typical, you have so little silence you don't know what to do—and especially when you're in a room with other people. Noise tends to cover the shallowness.

Can you picture a typical evening at home for the family? The husband lounges on the sofa as he flicks from one channel to another. His wife sits across the room chatting on the phone. As soon as she finishes one call, another comes in or she thinks of one she needs to return. Their teenaged children are being influenced by people on the corner. While the productivity and the sharpening of your skills could be taking place, you're too busy being entertained and distracted.

Yes, noise does cover up shallowness. In fact, I'll say it this way. Growing closer to God means you will need and you will demand silent times just for you and God. The closer you grow toward God you not only learn to tolerate silence, but you learn to embrace it. It's the time when your spiritual ears are tuned to God's channel.

I challenge you, and may the Holy Ghost arrest your attention and help you shift your lifestyle so that you no longer conform. May the Lord truly help you not only to listen but to yearn to listen. May God cause you to hunger and thirst for divine solitude so that you no longer hear the distractions and the noise.

If you want to hear from God, remind yourself that God isn't going to shout.

He does His best speaking in whispers.

He does it even better in silence.

60 SECONDS TO THINK

1. What is the single biggest distraction in your life?

2. What is one thing you can do to overcome that distraction?

3. Dr. Robert Schuller chose to fail at one thing: returning phone calls. What one thing can you choose to fail to do? If you fail to do that one thing, what will it enable you to do?

4. Read these words aloud: "Don't copy the behavior and customs of this world, but let God transform you into a new person by changing the way you think" (Romans 12:2, NLT). What does that verse say to you? What distractions actually cause you to copy the behavior and customs of the world?

5. Are you afraid of silence? Does silence itself become a distraction for you? Ponder that question for 60 seconds and decide what you can do to embrace the silence and not fight it.

18

60 SECONDS FOR

Your Health

"God has called her home to be with Him," I said at a recent funeral. That was true but it was also a lie. God accepted her and maybe God did call her home. But if He did, it was because she ate herself to death.

It's amazing how many people are prematurely being planted in boxes because they won't change their lifestyles, and it's not because of ignorance. They're so caught up in eating and lying around that they forget (or won't admit) that God created the body to function like a machine. To work well, the body needs to move. We call that exercise.

To make it worse, I have to hear all the jokes about, "Yes, I'm eating myself to death but it's a wonderful way to go."

Really?

It may seem like that at the moment, but I have sad, sad news for people who make such jokes. I think it's a way of pushing away guilt, of denying what they're doing, and hiding from the truth. They remind me of the people a decade ago who puffed away on their cigarettes and talked about how much pleasure it gave them. They didn't count on the health problems they would have a few years later such as lung cancer, heart problems, and emphysema.

This is a big issue for Christians today, and especially in America. We're the fattest people on earth and we're getting fatter. (However, recent reports say the Brits are on their way to be as fat and out of shape as we are.) When people visit the USA from other countries one of the things they often comment on is how fat Americans are. We really are the fattest people in the world. And the reasons aren't all glandular.

I've conducted too many funerals that took place because of preventable diseases. The deceased lived carelessly and conformed to the world around them as much as anyone else. When they got really sick, they expected a miracle. They left God out of their health when it was good, and pleaded for God to have mercy when it was bad. That doesn't make a lot of sense to me.

Those people ate nothing nutritious, worried about whether their health insurance would take care of them, stopped walking and moving around. They allowed their health to deteriorate when God had a better plan for them. They dishonored God by the way they lived. They died unfinished.

Does that sound harsh? I hope it sounds more like a warning. Many of those I've buried left this earth with their work and purpose unfinished. They left many loved ones behind: their children, spouse, and close friends. It was mean and selfish of them to have died unfinished when their passing could have been prevented or at least forestalled. If they had changed their eating habits and paid attention to their health, they could not only have extended their years, but they could have extended good health. They could have enjoyed their last years and been a blessing to others.

Everyone will die; that's not an issue. But how you live that last ten to fifteen years is up to you. You make lifestyle choices every day. Each time you choose to ignore your body, deny that it makes any difference what you do, or give in to bigger portions of food, you're choosing to die early. When you complain about the burden of exercise and taking care of your body, or you moan, "I know I need to exercise, but my life is too busy," you're choosing something else over your own well-being.

Keep it up: You're pushing toward an early grave. If your life is too busy now, the day will come when it won't be too busy. You'll be lying in bed unable to take care of your body. You made those choices years ago and now you're being rewarded for your efforts or lack of them.

Isn't it time that God's people change the world into a healthier, better place to live? Isn't it time that Christians honor their bodies and thus honor God? Not to honor our bodies is to dishonor the Creator. God has given us all kinds of great food and provided us with wisdom and common sense so that we can live great lives and be able to keep our earth suits intact to carry our spirit until God truly calls us home. He calls us home when we've completed our earthly assignment.

It's sad to say I find that most people who are passing away are passing prematurely, *and they are passing away full.* Not only full in their intestines with food that's not digested and stuck in their colon, but also full of unfulfilled destiny and filled with blessings they should have given to others. They had blessings for others that won't ever be received because they were selfish. They catered to their own immediate comfort. They wouldn't make changes. They wouldn't commit to live.

How do you make your lifestyle fit with Jesus' statement that He came to give us a life of abundance? (See John 10:10.) What scares me about that statement is that at the same time you can have both joy and abundance, but He puts in a condition—you might have it, or you may not have it—it's for you to choose.

I can write all of this, but I have serious struggles as well. I'm going to make a confession. Don't tell CNN or Larry King. Just keep this quiet and between us. I've been trying to lose weight for years, but I won't get on a scale because I don't want to know what I weigh now.

I've been on a diet for nearly four years. I still won't get on the scale because I'm afraid of where I am, and because I won't get on the scale I'm not losing any weight. I can tell that is reality and I don't have to get on the scale to prove it. I know it when I try to put on clothes that used to fit me. No matter how much I try to suck in my stomach, I can't get my pants to close.

Eventually I'll have to get on the scale and face the reality that I might be slightly overweight (or more than slightly). I know that once I face that truth, I'll also know the exact number of pounds I have to shed. Once I know both of those figures I can set up a new, effective plan for weight reduction. But one thing holds me back: I don't know how much I actually weigh. My scales are waiting to tell me.

Now I've confessed, and that means I need to do something to make changes. Just telling the world should be enough to push me to make changes. Remember accountability?

*   *   *

Through my own experience, I can tell you that in dealing with health issues, you also have to know about generations. There's a good chance you'll be susceptible to many of the same health problems as your parents or grandparents. For example, my father had all kinds of physical problems. He had high blood pressure and he was a diabetic. He also had prostate cancer, which is what caused his death.

Because of our father, my brothers and I started to get exams by the time we were in our late forties. A few years ago I learned that my oldest brother had prostate cancer. My next-to-oldest brother had prostate cancer that he did not get checked and it spread beyond his prostate. He struggled along for years fighting cancer. Finally it reached the point where we all were sure he was going to die. But God is still merciful. We prayed fervently for him and God healed him and turned everything around.

I vividly remember the day when I went and had myself checked. The doctor took a biopsy. A week later I went back for the results. The doctor looked straight at me and said, "You have prostate cancer."

I heard his words but they just kind of glazed over my head. "Okay," I said. "We'll talk later." I walked out in a daze because I didn't want to absorb what he said. But I had to face the reality: I had prostate cancer.

We did talk later and I went through a process of radiation and seed implant and I came out fine. The exams had detected it early enough. But what if I had not taken the opportunity to get checked? What if I had ignored the words of the doctor and done nothing?

I could have been unfair to my loved ones, my spouse, and my children because I ignored my health.

Health is important and that cancer became my wake-up call to life. Since then I've changed my diet. I've started to eat more fruits and vegetables and put into my system the things that will keep me healthy. I'm doing everything I can to fight off the tendencies I have for generational sickness. I want to break the generational physical curse in my bloodline. If I fight it by changing my lifestyle, I can also train my children so they can fight it as well.

I tell people, "This isn't just about you and your health. It's also about the people who love you. It's about being obedient to God and treating your body as a temple of God. It's about being healthy and staying around for others."

When I was coming up we didn't hear much about cancer. We'd hear once every ten years or so that some very old person had died of cancer. But they had already lived a pretty good life.

When I was coming up, Mama cooked everything from our garden. We ate pinto beans, cornbread (and I mean real cornbread). Mama cooked real food every day. We didn't question our health much because we had good health.

That's not true in our world today. The Centers for Disease Control and Prevention (CDC) announced a few years ago that nearly two-thirds of Americans are overweight and of that group, a third of them are moribund obese. Our children eat trash. They become chemically addicted to additives. That's why they're developing diabetes, cancer, tumors—yes, even our children—and they think they're all right because they're young and strong. The CDC said that a record number of children—kids under the age of twelve—have developed what they call type 2 diabetes. They used to call it adult-onset diabetes because only adults, and usually those over age fifty, had it. No longer is it limited to older adults. This is just as true with heart trouble and hypertension.

And it's preventable!

The worst information provided by research is about our children—the upcoming generation. Someone said to me, "They may live longer than our generation, but they won't live healthier. They'll have medicines and surgical procedures to keep them alive, but they won't enjoy their days. They'll be too sick."

He may be right.

On July 16, 2003, Richard H. Carmona, Surgeon General of the United States, spoke on "The Obesity Crisis in America." He made it clear that obesity is a crisis and called it the fastest-growing cause of disease and death in America. He also said it's completely preventable. Among other things, he pointed out that one out of every eight deaths in America is caused by an illness directly related to overweight and obesity. He emphasized that our children are already seeing the initial consequences of a lack of physical activity and unhealthy eating habits. His words sent out a challenge and a warning that we need to change our ways.

If enough voices cry out, maybe the message will take hold. I'm not a doctor and this isn't a medical lecture; however, this is common information everyone needs to know. These aren't facts hidden away in some obscure medical journal. These are facts we can find almost everywhere. I've done a little reading on the topic of obesity and consulted with a few experts. They call obesity a chronic condition (or maybe we should say permanent) and it means people have an excessive amount of body fat and it's not going to go away without drastic life changes.

Although reports vary, the general consensus is that about three hundred thousand deaths in the United States every year are the result of obesity. This condition isn't just about looks. Obesity also increases the risk of developing a number of chronic diseases, including insulin resistance, high blood pressure (hypertension), strokes (cerebrovascular accident or CVA), heart attacks, congestive heart failure, various types of cancer, gallstones, gout, osteoarthritis (degenerative arthritis), and sleep apnea.

Why should that surprise anyone? We've raised a generation of fast-food, grease-and-processed-chicken eaters. Some birds have never moved more than a few inches in their entire lives. They're thrown into overcrowded pens and fed food to make them fat. There have been reported cases of steroid additives being injected into their feed. That means that whatever those chickens take into their bodies stays inside and is passed on to humans.

Caloric intake is rising while physical activity is declining. And when it comes to dinnertime, we're opting for speed and convenience over nutrition. I've read that 40 percent of the American family food budget is spent away from home in restaurants, on fast food, and on meals bought through food services.

This has to change. And the change has to start with each person who reads this book. *You* need to make drastic lifestyle changes within the family or many of you will bury your own children. Your kids are now experiencing heart attacks before they're old enough to vote. High blood pressure has trickled down to affect teens. Your kids receive medication of almost every kind. Schoolteachers will tell you that the number of kids in their classes on Ritalin or something else overwhelms them.

All of us need to make changes. We can't wait for the Food and Drug Administration to do it or for school districts to act. We have to do things to take charge of our health and the health of our children.

I could go on and on but I hope I've made my point. Our kids are sick and afflicted with what used to be age-related diseases. By the time they're thirty, they've developed the diseases that people twice their age encountered. If you're a typical American, you also need to make lifestyle changes. You need to make those serious changes so you can help change your children and your children's children. As you change, they can see the need to change.

I'm not trying to set up a diet plan for anyone, but here are a few tips I've picked up from reading and from talking to experts about weight control. This information came from a book called *Live 10 Healthy Years Longer* by Dr. Jan Kuzma and Cecil Murphey. The material in the book is based on forty years of research done by the National Institutes of Health and Loma Linda University (California).* Dr. Kuzma was head of the program for twenty-five of those years.

---

* *Live 10 Healthy Years Longer* by Jan W. Kuzma and Cecil Murphey (Waco, Texas: Word Publishing, 2000), pages 2–4.

1. **Eat slowly and enjoy your food.** When you're feeling pressured, your overloaded system doesn't handle digestion properly. Some complain that they don't have time to eat leisurely meals. That's reason enough to relax and eat slowly. If you have only a limited amount of time, it's better to eat less than it is to gulp down your food.

   People who eat slowly tend to eat less. It's one way to limit the quantity of food. The more you eat, the more the digestive system has to work.

2. **Chew thoroughly.** The digestive process begins in the mouth, not the stomach. By chewing your food longer, you prepare your food with more salivary amylase (enzymes needed for better processing in the stomach, which is a kind of predigesting process).

3. **The closer to the natural state, the more nutritious the food, and the more you will need to chew.** Those who eat a lot of raw and unprocessed foods tend to enjoy better health.

4. **Limit the variety of food you eat at each meal.** Keep it simple. Three or four separate dishes are enough variety for most people. Some have found success by making a habit of *not* serving food in courses. They say it's easy to overeat if you don't think about how much is yet to come.

5. **Exercise moderately after meals.** Many of us can remember eating a heavy lunch and having to sit in a classroom or meeting. Our minds probably felt dull for an hour or so. We may even have fallen asleep. Too much food dulls mental activity and blunts the memory and perceptive faculties.

6. **Avoid eating immediately after heavy exertion.** Digestion demands more from your system than most of us realize. Heavy exercise just before a meal may prevent your digestive organs from getting the resources they need. It is better if you can allow a little time to relax before eating.

7. **Space meals five or six hours apart.** Don't eat until your stomach has had a chance to rest from the hard labor of digesting the previous meal. Many of those who have trouble spacing out eating have learned to drink a lot of water between meals. Not only is it healthful, but drinking one or two glasses of water can also fool our bodies into thinking we're not hungry. This makes the stomach feel full without adding calories to digest.

8. **Consider eating two meals a day.** Some have found this works best for shedding pounds. Others, as they grow older, see eliminating one meal as a way to prevent weight gain. It's not the lifestyle for everyone.

    When most people decide to eat only two meals a day, they usually cut breakfast. But that's the one meal *not* to avoid. In fact, the experts seem unanimous that we should make breakfast the *largest* meal of the day. Our bodies need more food at the start of the workday than at the end. The meal to skip is in the evening.

9. **Eat meals at regular hours.** Our bodies readily adapt to cycles and rhythms, and they function best when events such as meals come at regular, fixed times each day. Initially, some people may experience discomfort in making this change, but our bodies adjust after a few attempts.

* * *

The real question is this: How important is your health? You probably don't think much about your body as long as you're doing all right. But once disease starts to set in, you get concerned about your body. But suppose you decided to take seriously the reality that your body doesn't belong to you? What if you thought of your body as being on loan to you from God? It has been "leased" to you for your lifetime on earth. When you stand before our Lord and Creator, one of the things you'll have to do is to give an accounting of how you treated the leased body. Paul refers to the body as a holy temple and urges us to care for it.

- "Do you not know that you are the temple of God and that the Spirit of God dwells in you? If anyone defiles the temple of God, God will destroy him. For the temple of God is holy, which temple you are" (1 Corinthians 3:16–17).

- "Or do you not know that your body is the temple of the Holy Spirit who is in you, whom you have from God, and you are not your own? For you were bought at a price, therefore glorify God in your body and in your spirit, which are God's" (1 Corinthians 6:19–20).

- "I plead with you to give your bodies to God because of all he has done for you. Let them be a living and holy sacrifice—the kind he will find acceptable. This is truly the way to worship him" (Romans 12:1, NLT).

If you seriously and faithfully accept those biblical statements and determine to do something about them, you can change. Romans 12:2 goes on to exhort, "Don't copy the behavior and customs of this world, but let God transform you into a new person by changing the way you think" (NLT). The change begins in the head. You have to rethink your health. Years ago, the writer Charlie Shedd wrote a book called *The Fat Is in Your Head*. He wrote it as a man who had gone on countless diets until he figured out he needed to change his thinking instead of just counting calories.

Please make changes. Treat your body as God intended it to be honored: Treat it as a holy temple. Make changes so you can live and enjoy the abundant life. But also do it for your children. Leave them a living example of someone who lived a full *and healthy life*, and that can be part of your lasting legacy to them.

The health crisis is more than a weight issue. New studies come out regularly that tell you that you probably don't get enough exercise. I can only plead with every reader to get into an exercise program that suits you. It can be as easy as fast-paced walking at least four times a week. Get the heart rate up. Find something that you enjoy doing as exercise and stick with it. Get a friend to go on an exercise program with you.

It's now fairly well known that kids who play vigorously for twenty to forty minutes each day are better able to organize their schoolwork and get better grades. That sounds like a strong reason to push kids to exercise their bodies. Better yet, get your kids to exercise with you. You'll both be benefitting your health and you'll get to spend some quality time together. And you'll be acting as a role model for your children.

When my cowriter was forty, his blood pressure was right at the high-level range. Both his parents had high blood pressure and his father died of a stroke. He was about twenty-five pounds overweight. After a routine physical, his doctor said, "If your blood pressure goes any higher, you'll need to go on medication."

"I knew about exercise and nutrition but I hadn't done anything to change," he said. "I had no physical problems before the blood pressure, but I knew I had to make changes." He learned about nutrition and better eating habits.

He decided to run regularly. To stay with it, he persuaded three friends to run with him three mornings a week. One of them dropped out after two weeks and a second one after about a month. One of the men ran with him until they had built up a distance of four miles. Today he runs alone about thirty miles a week. He's also quick to say, "Running is not for everyone. Find out what physical action you like and go for it."

Another issue you don't hear much about is sleep. Americans pride themselves on getting the fewest hours of sleep. As someone told me, "For most men, sleeping is a feminine act. True men feel they have to overcome the desire to sleep."

The reality is that sleep is a physical need. You need sleep, and most people need at least seven hours. Seven to nine hours is the normal amount that experts agree on. What the experts often don't point out is that sleep time is when the body repairs itself from day-to-day wear. If you don't get adequate sleep, your body doesn't get the needed repairs. Do you get enough sleep? Most Americans don't. They try to cheat themselves and think they can get away with something. They don't.

An article in *USA Today* reported on a study based on door-to-door surveys of 87,000 American adults by the National Center for

Health Statistics. They reported that those who "sleep fewer than six hours a night—or more than nine—are more likely to be obese"*

The study also linked weight to other studies that have found obesity and other health problems with those who don't get proper sleep.

A physician friend once told me, "You can mistreat your body only so long and deprive yourself of sleep for a time, but one day, the body rebels. You get sick. You lose work and maybe even end up in the hospital. Is it worth it?"

Isn't it better to treat our bodies as God's temple and take care of them so that we can honor God by the way we take care of our bodies?

When was the last time you honored the Sabbath? Sabbath is the day God rested after six days of creation. It's the day He set apart for the Jews to rest from their labors, according to the command in Exodus 20:8–11. If you read through the Old Testament, you see that the desecration of the Sabbath was a constant cry from the prophets and priests.

It's more than just observing a rigid Old Testament law. Jesus said that the Sabbath law was made for us. (See Mark 2:27.) God gave you a day of rest because your body needs it. To talk about observing the Sabbath today almost sounds laughable, but research backs up the benefits. Rest your body. Rest it and it functions better.

Another way to increase your health is to develop a positive at-

* *USA Today,* May 8, 2008, page 4D.

titude. The research seems endless to prove what a wise man said centuries ago: "A merry heart does good, like medicine, But a broken spirit dries the bones" (Proverbs 17:22).

Every area of your life is important. And you need to pay attention and perhaps make changes. To help you make changes in your lifestyle, I want to suggest a few things.

First, remind yourself that your body doesn't belong to you. It's God's property. You have it on lease.

Second, ask yourself this question: "If I could make a few changes in my diet and lifestyle *and add a dozen healthy years* to my life, would I be willing to do it?"

Third, this isn't just about food and exercise. This is about every area of your life.

Take 60 seconds for one of the most important decisions you need to make in this life. Take those seconds to think about how to balance your life. Part of that balance will be to change the way you eat, to decide to exercise, and to change your way of thinking.

In 2005, the government set up new guidelines that advise thirty minutes of exercise on most days. They urged Americans to maintain a healthy weight. In addition, they advised:

- Eat a variety of nutrient-dense foods from the basic food groups—grains, fruits, vegetables, dairy, and meats.

- Choose meat, poultry, dry beans, and milk products that are lean, low fat or fat free.

- Keep consumption of fat to between 20 and 35 percent of your daily calories, with most coming from sources of polyunsaturated and monounsaturated fats, such as fish, nuts, and vegetable oils. Limit intake of saturated and trans fats, cholesterol, added sugars, and caloric sweeteners.

• Consume less than one teaspoon of salt a day.

Most of us were born with the birthright to enjoy good health and a sense of well-being. Through our choices, frequently influenced by our peers and the media, we decide either to maintain this birthright or to give it up. Too often we accept the fatalistic view that it's normal to have a heart attack or stroke. *It's not normal.* We can prevent those fatal illnesses, especially those that strike in middle age.

Think carefully about having an extra decade of life—ten more years of active, healthy life. How much effort would you put into your day-to-day living if you knew it would pay off in less pain, fewer illnesses, a minimal amount of worry, and a more positive outlook on life?

Before you answer that question, I want to assure you that I don't suggest you jump into an exercise program of jerking, bouncing, and kicking gyrations. The experts don't advocate a highly restrictive eating program of tasteless, boring choices. If you follow the right example and learn to eat more healthful foods, you can live longer and enjoy your life more. *Isn't that good news?*

Here's another bit of good news about individuals who live happier lives: They don't diet. According to the study by the NIH and Loma Linda University, those who ate healthful food had fewer weight problems than the general population. *They don't diet because they don't need to.* Sensible eating habits regulated their weight.

Wouldn't it be more fun to be in charge of your life? To learn to live by *principles* of good nutrition instead of slavishly following rules?

It can happen!

You can live more healthy, happy years. If you do, you honor God, who created you. You honor God and you honor your family by staying longer on this earth to be with them. Isn't it worth it to make changes in your lifestyle?

60 SECONDS TO THINK

1. Take 60 seconds and look at your body. Stand alone in front of a mirror. Ask yourself these questions: "Does my body glorify God? Do I honor God's temple by the way I live?" If not, confess it and ask for God's help.

2. If you're not getting enough sleep, what can you do to give your temple the rest it needs?

3. Ask yourself: "If I decided to change my lifestyle, what is the first thing I would need to do to treat my body properly?"

4. What will I have to do to develop an exercise program and a balanced diet? What is the first step I need to take?

19

Leave a Legacy

In the Old Testament God identifies Himself as the God of Abraham, Isaac, and Jacob. That makes us realize that an important element in the Old Testament is the generational legacy. They didn't think so much of eternal life and what happened after death. They thought of their legacy of influencing the generations that followed them.

Think about the legacy of Joseph. Joseph didn't just arise one day and decide, "I have nothing else important going on today so I'll get things in order so I can leave a large, lasting legacy to the world." There had to be a process. He could leave a powerful legacy because he lived faithfully and he died with no regrets. He blessed his children and his children's generation.

Or think about Joshua, who was Moses' right-hand man and his successor. Near the end of his life, when Joshua was 110 years old, he called together the leaders of Israel and urged them to be faithful to God. After he died, the Bible records his legacy: "Israel served the LORD all the days of Joshua, and all the days of the elders who outlived Joshua, who had known all the works of the LORD which He had done for Israel" (Joshua 24:31).

In the Old Testament period, the people recognized and valued the wise (and they were usually individuals with gray hair). They sat at the gates of the city and people with problems could come to them and talk to them. They shared their wisdom and taught them.

That was their legacy for those who followed. People realized that the seniors who sat at the gate had been around a long time, knew the mistakes (made some of them themselves), and could save a lot of heartache if the younger generation listened to them.

One of the things that disturbs me today is that we don't have a minute to pause and to listen to the elders who sit at the gate. In our present day, nobody sits on the porch as they did when I was a boy. There's nobody who has time to talk to another generation.

Instead, everything we teach has to be formalized. When I was coming up I walked down to the corner store or through the neighborhood and someone would be there. They would talk to me and I listened. They didn't have a degree, but they'd been through some hard life and they knew what they were talking about. More than one person said to me, "Eddie, you listen to me, boy. You'd better quit that or you'll be sorry." Others would pull me aside and stare into my eyes and say, "Boy, you're somebody. You don't need to be doing that."

And I straightened up.

Poor Jacob's story takes place at the time in his life when he should have enjoyed his wisdom and walked in fellowship with

God. But he says his remaining sons can't comfort him and he plans to go to the grave mourning for his lost son, Joseph.

Jacob had his conversion experience, or at least we think he did. We know he wrestled with God. By then, his children were already born and most of them were grown. Joseph was six years old. This means that during the important, formative years of his children's lives they did not see him as Israel. They did not see him as a worshiper. They did not see him as one who sat at the gate of integrity. It was just too late because he had taught them his old ways and that's what they followed. If you don't start working on children when they're still young, you lose your chance. They need to know the Scriptures and to hear them when they're young. They need your wisdom now.

I once read about a woman who came to a famous teacher and brought along her son. "When should I start teaching him?" she asked.

"How old is he?"

"Just six."

"Rush home," he said. "Get busy. You've lost the best six years of his life."

True story or not, we now know that we influence our children most during those years before they reach seven. A century ago the Jesuits used to say, "Give me your child until he's seven years old, and he'll never leave the church." That may be an exaggeration, but the principle is correct. The basic personality traits of your son and daughter are established between the ages of four and six. And after that they'll spend the rest of their life trying to change what was ingrained in them.

If you wasted precious moments working two jobs or getting heavily into debt, and your children became MTV babies, that's the way you've taught them. You've pursued money, and babysitters became their parents. Whoever rocks the cradle gets their ear.

But imagine yourself lying in bed during your senior years, reflecting and reading back through the chapters of your life story. I want you to imagine what that would be like.

Ask yourself:

- What did my life add up to?

- What did I live for?

- Who will remember me?

- What will they say about me after I'm dead?

- Was it important that I existed? What did I contribute to the world?

It's the old saying of having so many questions and only so much time. Will you be able to lie in the bed with no regrets? Some regrets? Nothing but regrets?

What an agonizing moment to find yourself in ... there you are in the sunset of your life, full of regrets, finally seeing the picture, but it's too late to change it. And the awesome additional tragedy of it is that it wasn't just about you. Because you didn't live right, your lifestyle cursed others.

Everybody ends up somewhere. But few people end up somewhere on purpose. *You* are going to end up somewhere. Either you're going to choose where you end up or life is going to choose the place for you. It's like getting on the bus and missing your stop and getting dropped off somewhere that has nothing to do with where you wanted to go.

The great news is that anyone can discover the meaningful life direction. Everyone can end up somewhere on purpose. The Bible makes it clear that we are designed to live a unique life for a reason: for a dream, for a big idea, for a personal mission. That is because you and I are made in His image.

Isaiah 46:10 says, "Declaring the end from the beginning, And from ancient times things that are not yet done, Saying, 'My counsel shall stand, And I will do all My pleasure.'" Psalm 139:13–16 tells us, "For You formed my inward parts; You covered me in my mother's womb. I will praise You, for I am fearfully and wonderfully made; Marvelous are Your works, And that my soul knows very well. My frame was not hidden from You, When I was made in secret, And skillfully wrought in the lowest parts of the earth. Your eyes saw my substance, being yet unformed. And in Your book they all were written, The days fashioned for me, When as yet there were none of them."

Think of those words: The days were fashioned for you *before* there were any days. Too often we think life just happens, but we need to understand that God designed the day for you. That is the reason He says, "In all your ways acknowledge Him, And He shall direct your paths" (Proverbs 3:6).

Why does God say that? Because He has already directed your way. That is the reason Jesus said, "... seek first the kingdom of God and His righteousness, and all these things shall be added to you"

(Matthew 6:33). Why did he say that? Because your day had already been fashioned before there was a day and when you follow God and make Him first, He's ready to bless you.

Proverbs 29:18 says, "Where there is no vision, the people perish" (KJV). Where there is no dream, no redemptive revelation, no vision, no sense of creative purpose, we perish. Where there is no vision that you were created to have a growing, lifelong, and personal relationship with your Creator, your inner being withers and dies.

Where there is no vision for a godly family, you have a 50 percent chance of ending up in divorce. Where there is no vision that your body is the temple of God, the property on loan from Him, your physical health will slip away and you will start to fade. Where there is no vision for your financially stable lifestyle, you can live in the richest country in the world and still live broke and jacked up. Where there is no vision for meaningful work in people's lives, they find that all they do is wake up and work to get to five o'clock so they can go home.

Whenever the topic of legacy comes up, I don't think many of us take it seriously. A lot of us think of famous people and what they left, not realizing that everyone leaves a legacy. *Everyone,* whether it is a good one or whether it is bad, we leave a legacy. It's what we hand down to the next generation and the generation after that. This can include money and possessions, but it's much, much more than that.

Many of us never plan for those who follow. Whatever we leave behind just happens that way. Don't let it just happen to you. I challenge you to take it seriously—this is important.

The legacy you leave is one of the most important things in your life.

Many of you started out hard in life because there was no encouraging or helpful legacy prepared for you. You had no shoulders to stand on to reach higher. You started with nothing and you had to build everything. Don't follow that pattern and die leaving nothing for someone else.

It's unfair. It's also selfish. If you care about those who follow, you'll do what you can to make life easier for them. This is God's plan for you and for all of us.

God wants each generation to leave a legacy for those who follow. One translation from the Psalms says this:

O my people, listen to my instructions. Open your ears to what I am saying . . . I will teach you hidden lessons from our past—stories we have heard and known, stories our ancestors handed down to us. We will not hide these truths from our children; we will tell the next generation about the glorious deeds of the LORD, about his power and his mighty wonders . . . He commanded our ancestors to teach them to their children, so the next generation might know them—even the children not yet born—and they in turn will teach their own children. So each generation should set its hope anew on God, not forgetting his glorious miracles and obeying his commands. Then they will not be like their ancestors—stubborn, rebellious, and unfaithful, refusing to give their hearts to God (Psalm 78:1–8, NLT).

God lays it out clearly. Each generation is to leave a legacy for those who follow. Did you notice how many times the writer spoke about teaching and instructions? There's a reason: Good, rich legacies are no accident.

You need to be mindful of your daily living and ask yourself, "What am I leaving behind me? Is it good that my children and my children's children will imitate me?"

It scares me when I think of the way some will have to answer that question. I've met many people who I wouldn't call great in their day and many people don't even know their names today. But they remember what those individuals did. The present generation can look backward and give thanks for the foundation of high moral values and a desire to achieve.

To leave a good legacy is called finishing strong. That means you can get a great start, but if you don't do it right, if you don't slide into it, if you don't move in the things that build and if you make the bad moves at the end, you fizzle out. You're not remembered for your start, you're remembered for how you end. That's what they say about you and that's what they remember. Your generation, your bloodline is where it is, based off of the legacy that was built the generation before you.

Are you satisfied with what was built before? Are you contented with the direction you're going? If so, that's good news; continue on that path. But if you're not satisfied and you want to see your children's children, you need to make changes. It's not just your immediate bloodline but it involves others who are connected with you, so use *your* life as a springboard and a story to be told that will bring inspiration. You can become a blessing in your time and in the generations that follow if you deliberately live in such a way that you have built something to remain after you're gone.

Your legacy is what remains after you leave this earth. Make it powerful. Make it great. Make it to be remembered. Do that, and you will have accomplished kingdom business.

One of my mentors was Reverend Oddie Davis Brown. He pastored the Second Baptist Church in Richmond, Virginia, on the corner of Idlewood and Randolph Street. He has long since passed, but one of the things that made him great was that he always ministered from reality. He could see a stoplight and other simple objects and from them create powerful stories and lead us into reading the Bible. By his direct and simple way, he made the Bible alive and he dealt with the realities of life.

On any Sunday morning, the church would be packed and the balcony would overflow. That's because others received from him what I did. His messages captivated me and made me want to be a better and more faithful Christian.

At the end of each service he would say, "Remember to let go and let God." He wasn't just repeating a slogan from Alcoholics Anonymous. He was throwing out a powerful exhortation to each of us.

He passed suddenly at age fifty-seven, but he inspired me. He not only helped me to believe in God, he helped me to believe in myself, and enabled me to see that I had a destiny and a purpose.

I believe his legacy is one of the major reasons New Birth has grown and we have made an impact around the world. I face the same issues and problems everyone else faces, but I've never forgotten his exhortation to let go and let God. It was as if he imprinted those words on my brain. Oddie Davis Brown's ability to tap into reality and to be able to make the complex things seem so simple is a legacy that he left for me. Others have picked up and extended his legacy.

His powerful influence has allowed us to grow much bigger and touch more lives than he ever touched. His legacy reminds me of the words of Jesus who said, "He who receives you receives Me, and he who receives Me receives Him who sent Me" (Matthew 10:40). Jesus went on to point out that if we receive the righteous or give them even a cup of cold water, we share in the reward.

That's also part of the legacy. Because Oddie Davis Brown influenced me, part of whatever I receive as a reward for my faithfulness is also his. That's how it works. We learn from others and then we pass it on as our legacy. Oddie Davis Brown still touches me and I can pass it on. Even today, long after he's gone, his legacy grows and continues to bless folk.

For me, legacy means those rich, lasting inspirations that have altered lives for the better. Most people think about the famous, but I also include the not-so-famous. Heroes have been overrepresented in the fields of sports and entertainment. There are certainly positive people in those lines of work, but we need to bring our focus closer to Jesus. We need to look at those men and women, young and old, whose Christian lives we've been privileged to observe, and receive their influence.

Think of it this way: What you leave behind speaks more for you than what you say about yourself. People can see you in public and think one thing, but after you're gone, how will they see you? In another chapter I spoke about zeros or placeholders. Is that how you want to be remembered? Do you want to be remembered (if at all) as someone who lived, died, and didn't make much difference in life?

So you made some wrong choices? Perhaps part of your legacy will be that you started with a wasted or foolish life and turned it around. You changed and your example grew and became the influence and guiding light for those who follow. You start by facing those bad choices and then you forgive yourself.

The first basis for forgiveness is to look at your motives. Why did I do that? That's a good question to ask yourself. And the next thing to do is ask yourself if you're truly sorry for those mistakes or failures of judgment.

We're told all through the Bible that if we confess our sins, our faithful God forgives. (See 1 John 1:9.) I love Psalm 103:12–13, which says, "As far as the east is from the west, So far has He removed our transgressions from us. As a father pities his children, So the LORD pities those who fear Him."

If God forgives you, you can forgive yourself. Some folk are a lot meaner and tougher on themselves than God is. Look backward and forgive yourself even when you find out you were wrong. Determine not to repeat your mistakes.

Earlier in this book, I mentioned the three generations it took for the building and furnishing of a cathedral. Each generation did its part and left a glorious legacy for the generation that followed. I don't care what age you are, whether you're fifteen or fifty-five, the questions are still the same:

- What have you planted for your grandchildren?

- What do your grandchildren have in store for them because of your presence on this earth? It doesn't matter if you're not yet married or don't have grandchildren, you're still moving ahead.

- What have you put in line strategically for your grand-children?

"A good man leaves an inheritance to his children's children" (Proverbs 13:22). That's not by accident. It means that godly people think ahead and are concerned about their children and their children's children.

In another chapter I referred to Jacob when he was old. He grieved because he thought his favorite son, Joseph, was dead. His family surrounded him and wanted to bless him and encourage him. Jacob couldn't receive the blessing because he was in mourning. He mourned, I assume, because he looked at his children and realized they had picked up his bad attitude and lifestyle and not his good habits.

What a terrible place for a person to be near the end of life. To be older and watch your children and grandchildren make the same mistakes you did has to be discouraging. The problem with Jacob was that when his children were young and at a teachable age he was still a supplanter, a trickster, a deceiver, and he was involved in family strife. He could have been teaching his children to follow a different path.

It's no different today. We have so many family problems going on because nobody tries to reconcile. Everybody fights with someone else in the family and the children know about it. That also gives them permission, and they fight with their cousins and siblings. The only time they can get together is at funerals. They hate on each other while somebody lies in the box but that doesn't stop them from singing beautiful hymns.

It was too late for Jacob to be a good influence on his family. It's not too late for you. You can change now. Today.

As I think of the sad story of Jacob, I think of that oft-repeated phrase, "If I had known then what I know now . . ." The trouble is that when we finally say those words it's often too late. The opportunities for influence are fleeting. The generation coming after you needs to know that you don't have to rap or play sports to be successful. You need to show that to them now.

I can honestly say that I had a strong legacy to follow. I made mistakes, but I also remembered the values and attitudes my mama and my daddy taught me. They worked a plan. They discovered who they were and used their influence on my siblings and me. I'm a servant of God today because of them.

If you leave a good legacy, it begins with an authentic encounter with God. I don't mean emotion-charged worship or happy-sounding songs. They have a place. Some people tear up, but it's not the tears that move the heart of God. God is moved by a change of heart. God is moved when you say, "I was wrong. I was dead in sin. I need to change and I can't do it without Your help."

A hunger has to come from inside your soul. When that happens, God changes you. You are ready to leave a spiritual legacy.

While working on this book I was asked to do a home-going service for a gentleman who worked faithfully in our church. By his life and his godly example, he touched many lives. I wanted him to live forever, but he didn't. His days were numbered—just like the rest of us. I thank God that the man operated in a spirit of urgency so that he tried to bless and to enrich the lives of those he met each day. He left a legacy of greatness, not because he was famous, but because he was faithful and influenced the people around him.

Your days are numbered. People watch you because sometimes you're the only Bible they try to read. When you tell them you go to church they need to see more than a T-shirt and a bumper sticker. They need to see somebody who talks and acts differently. They need to see someone with a godly mind-set.

You need to be someone who says by your style of living, "I don't have a lot of time to waste, I don't have those minutes to hang with people who don't take me to the place I need to be. I have a sense of urgency, I've got some time to use up, a certain amount of time to do something."

If you're determined to leave a spiritual legacy, God will put an urgency in your spirit, which means you need wisdom to understand what you're to do in this moment and in each moment. God will show you the way.

60 SECONDS TO THINK

1. What kind of legacy do you want to leave your children and your children's children?

2. What kind of difference have you made by living on earth?

3. Think of one person who had a significant and positive influence on your life. What did that person do?

4. For the next 60 seconds, ponder this question: What must I do to leave a great legacy, a spiritual legacy, for those who follow me?

5. Write one thing you want your legacy to contain. For example, do you want to be remembered as someone who loved others? A person who prayed for others? Someone who held no malice against anyone?

20

Regret

What about you? When you look back over your life, what regrets will you have? Will you go to the grave sorrowing because of lost opportunities or because of doing the wrong things?

If you follow the things I've already laid out in this book, there should be no seconds left to regret. You've used your seconds and your minutes to turn your life around. You've made the right choices. You may not always see the results you wanted, but you'll know you did the right things at the right time.

Many of you will say you did the best you could at the moment. But as you learned more and as you've understood more of the ways of God, you realize you made mistakes. Go back and confess them. It's okay to say, "I said those things then, but God has given me more light and now I see things differently."

It takes courage to say, "I believed this five years ago. Now God has shown me where I was wrong and that wasn't the way to handle it. And I want to apologize and let you know where I am today."

Don't let pride hold you back. You can change and you can face reality from a new perspective. Why not change your thinking? Anyone can take a stand and refuse to change no matter what anyone says. I read recently that there are people who still believe the earth is flat. Despite the evidence, some insist the Holocaust never happened. I've even heard people question whether people have really traveled to the moon.

Purpose in your heart that you will not die with these words in your heart, "If only I had . . ."

60 SECONDS TO THINK

1. Will you be able to lie in your final bed with no regrets? Some regrets? Nothing but regrets?

2. What is one regret you feel right now? What can you do to overcome any regret you have?

3. What will you have to do to be able to say, "I have no regrets"?

4. Write these words: "I have forgiven myself for all the wrong choices I made. From this day onward, I will live the best way I can so that I can die with no regrets."

21

ON THE WAY TO

Greatness

I'm not perfect, as anyone who knows me will tell you. I'm far from a perfect role model. But I hope you'll overlook my human frailties and think of yourself and what you can become.

At times it may sound as if it's an easy task. It's not. In some ways you have to become like the salmon that swim upstream. You need to go against culture and fight off the easy way to do things. I heard that salmon make their way upstream by repeatedly bumping into blocked waterways until they find where the current is strongest and they have to fight to get there. Once there, it's still hard going, but their way is clear and they can focus on what's ahead. By facing both inner and outer adversities, you can maximize your life with a powerful momentum. You can give your all.

I called this book *60 Seconds to Greatness*. I mean that. You can be great in your life. Great doesn't mean being wealthy or being famous (although that's possible). Great means to maximize your life.

If you maximize your life, you'll develop your own Strategic Life Plan for the next hundred years. You'll follow it until Jesus calls you home. You will be a living example to those around you of God's greatness at work in you.

Be the best.

Be the greatest.

Be the best and the greatest you can be.

I'd like to hear from you once you've started on the way to greatness. I can't possibly answer every e-mail, but someone on my staff will help me with that. I want you to be great and I want to encourage you. Find my e-mail address on our website at http://www .newbirth.org/. Let my staff and me rejoice with you in your movement toward greatness.